THE BEST GNOME COLORING BOOK

VOL. 2

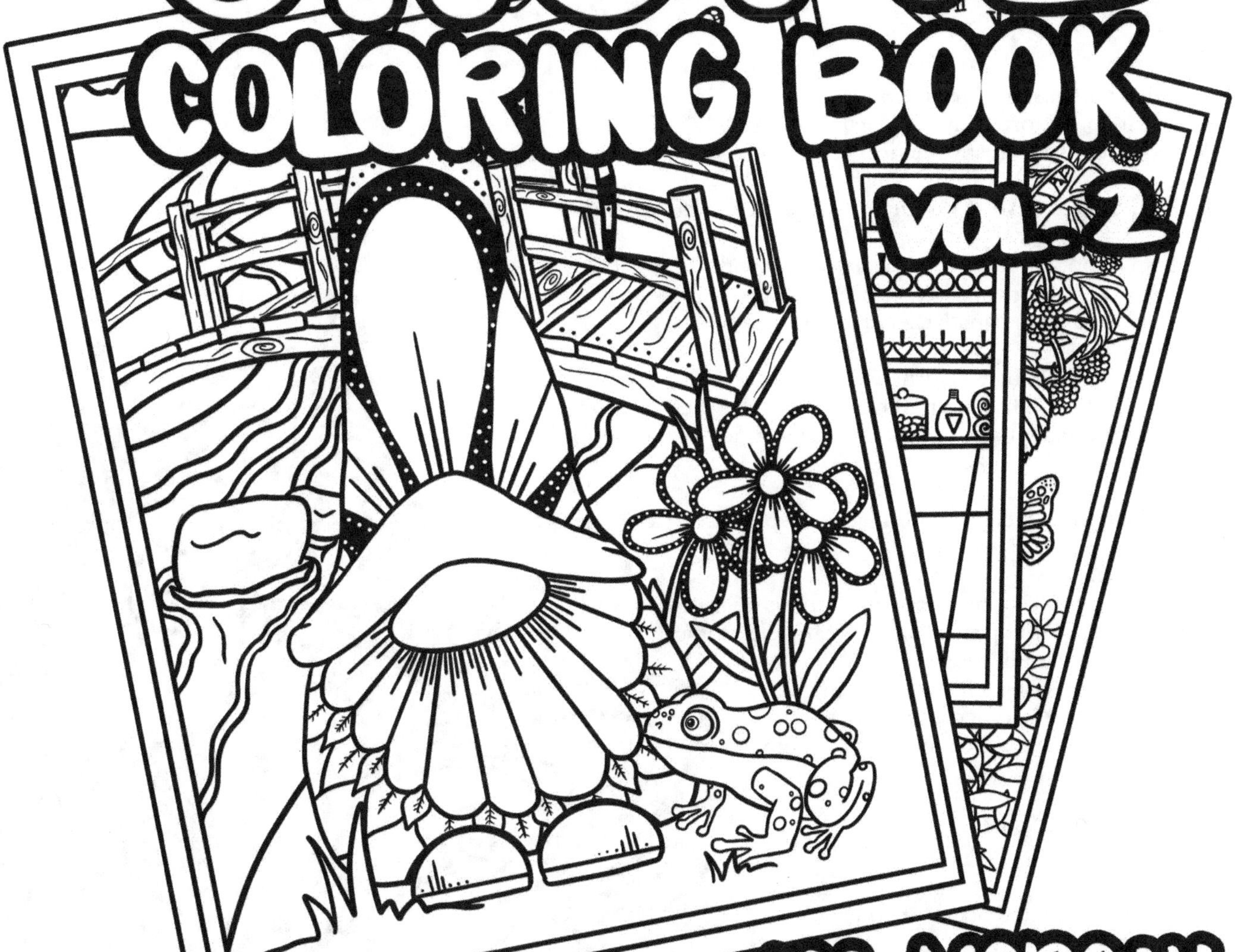

K.A. MORGAN

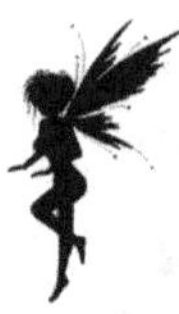

Inspire Books
A Division of Inspire Creative Services
937 West 1350 North, Clinton, Utah 84015, USA
kamorgan@inspirecreativeservices.com

THE BEST GNOME COLORING BOOK VOLUME TWO

An Inspire Book published by arrangement with the artist.

First Inspire Books paperback edition May, 2021

Cover Design by Kelli Ann Morgan at Inspire Creative Services

ISBN-13: 978-1-939049-57-5

Printed in the United States of America

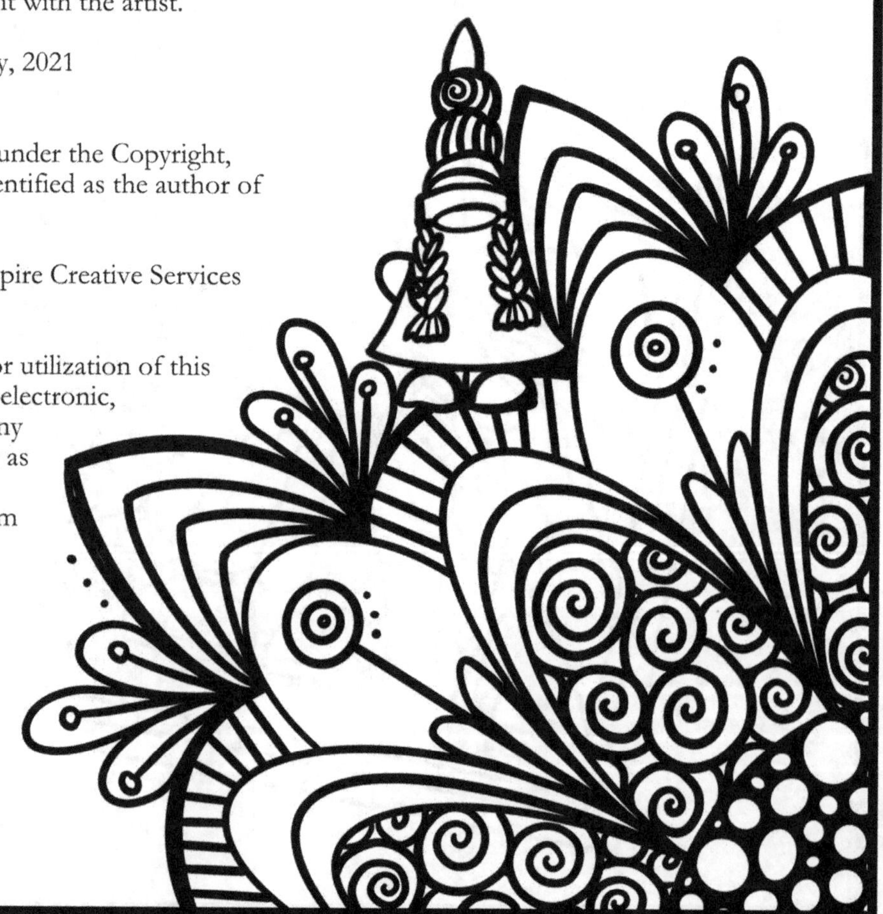

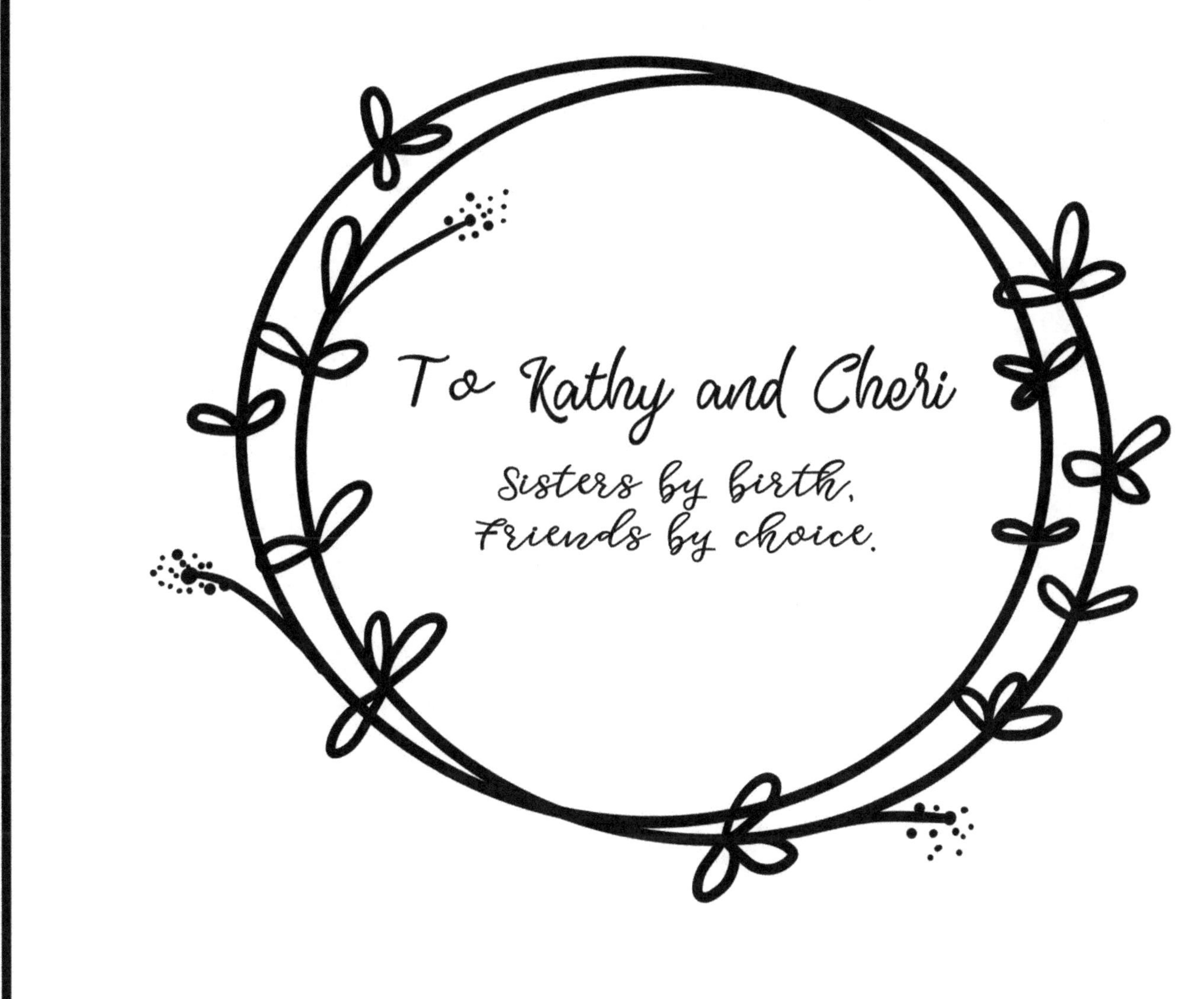
To Kathy and Cheri
Sisters by birth,
Friends by choice.

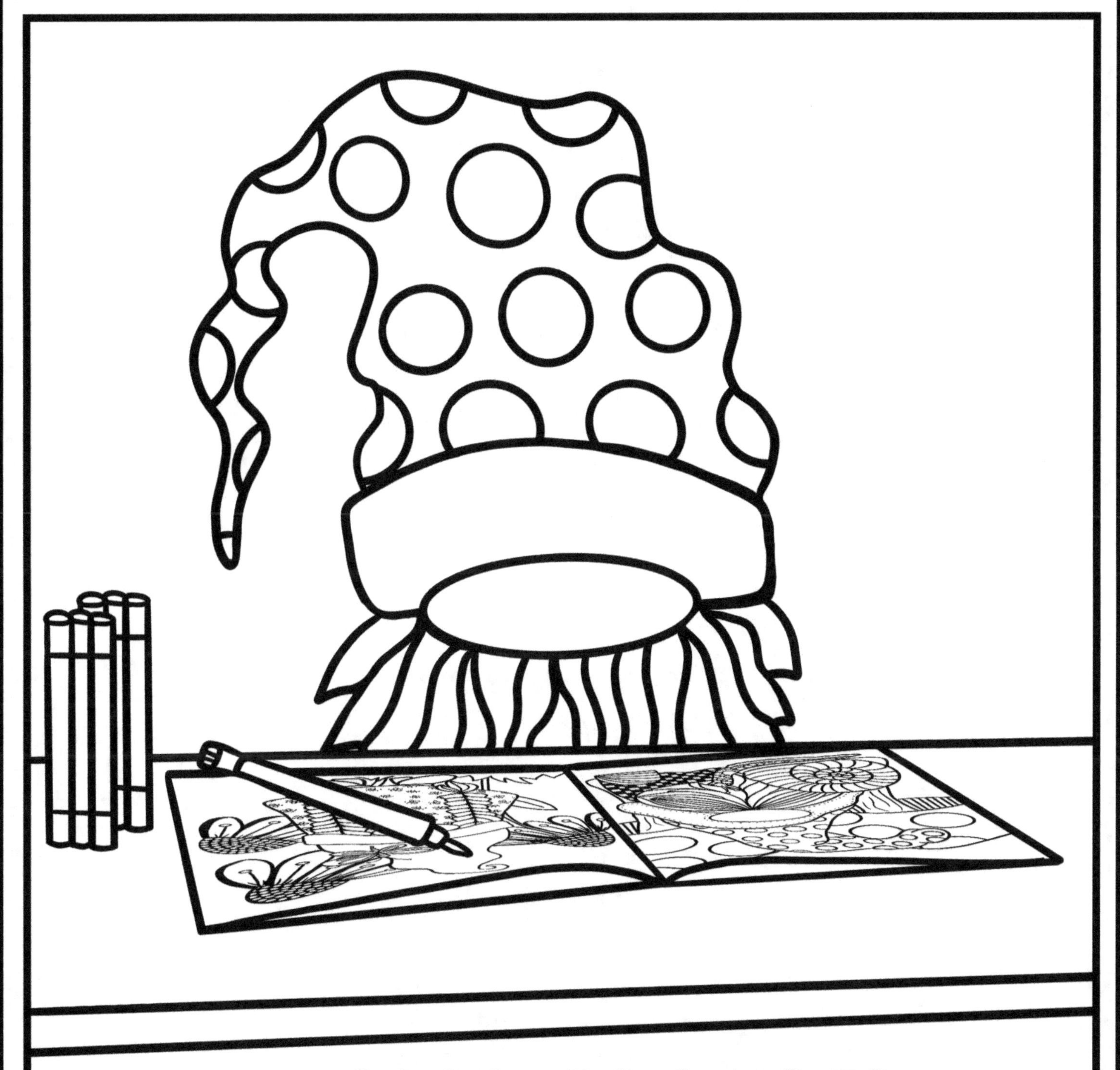

THIS BOOK BELONGS TO:

A NOTE FROM THE AUTHOR:

Thank you so much for purchasing THE BEST GNOME COLORING BOOK VOLUME ONE! Your support is invaluable.

I appreciate the opportunity to share my art with you and hope it will be a wellspring of creativity, healing, and relaxation.

Inspired by my handcrafted ceramic gnomes and fairy garden pieces, these whimsical designs came to life through my pen with the hope of bringing hours of enjoyment to both young and old(er) alike.

Whether you indulge in some much-needed alone time or build relationships with others as you spend time together, add your own personality to the page through color and unique embellishments. Have fun. Be happy. Forget your troubles for a time and remember that life is full of good things if you are willing to look for them.

Aside from art and graphic design, I also have a passion for writing, photography, pottery, music, board games, and spending time with the people I love most.

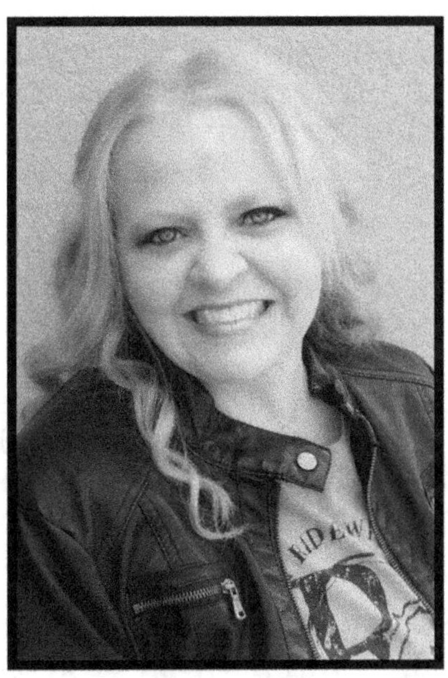

If you enjoyed this book, please leave a positive review on Amazon, Goodreads, Barnes & Noble or anywhere books are sold. Every voice counts and every review helps make it possible for me to continue producing more coloring books.

I would love to see your finished artwork. Please tag @kamorganbooks, use #kamorganbooks, or email me directly at kamorgan@inspirecreativeservices.com.

Thank you! And remember to always be kind!

Love,

Kelli Ann Morgan

COLORING TIPS:

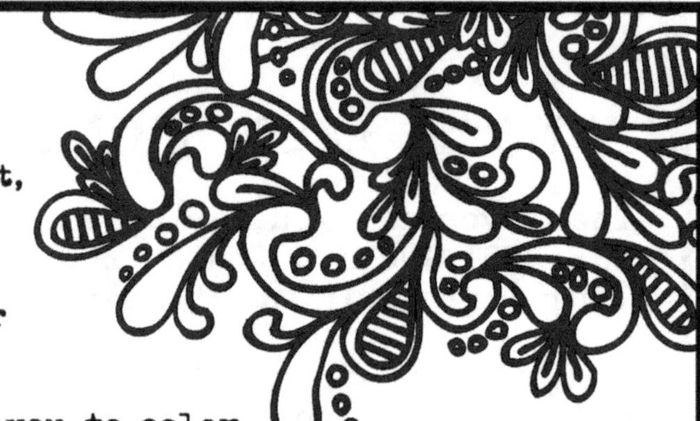

NOTE: If you are already a seasoned colorist, you likely will not need any of these tips, but for those who may just be starting or who may not color as often as you'd like, I hope these suggestions will help make your experience flawless and stress relieving.

1. Find a place that is comfortable for you to color and reduces distractions. (You may even want to set a relaxing mood with music, calming smells, etc...just make sure the area remains well lit.)

2. Choose your desired coloring page and select the appropriate color scheme and medium that speaks to you before you start coloring.

3. Use a black fine-point felt tip marker or pen to add your own designs or embellishments to the coloring page.

4. Use a white gel pen, white/light oil-based marker, or metallic marker to design on top of black or dark areas for highlights, added depth, dimension, and interest.

5. You do not have to color inside of the lines. In fact, you may choose to consistently color just outside of the line or to deliberately avoid coloring to the edge. However, if you do want to stay inside the lines, take a moment to outline the area to be colored first. (This is also a great technique to use when shading.)

6. Place a piece of cardstock or other paper behind the image you are coloring. If you are using markers, this will prevent colors from accidentally bleeding onto the next image. It also provides a surface with a little more give—making it so pens and pencils can glide more easily across the page.

7. If using alcohol markers, color the Color Test page before proceeding. The colors often appear differently on paper than the lid indicates.

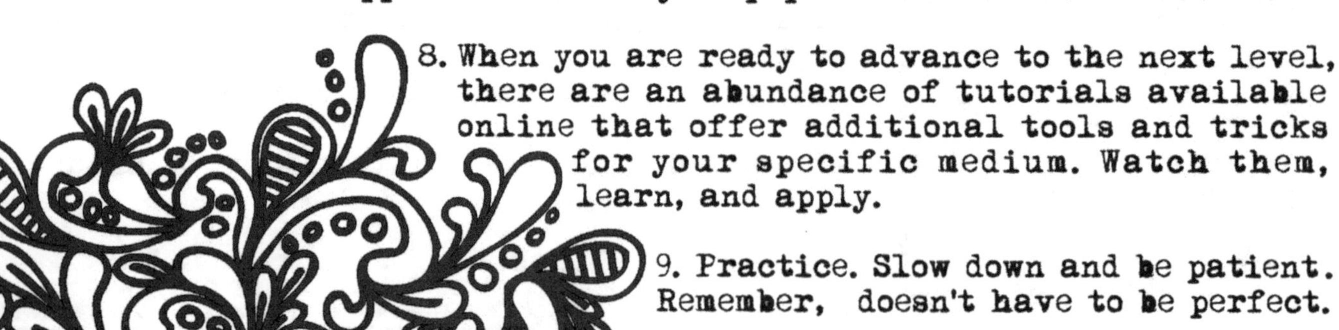

8. When you are ready to advance to the next level, there are an abundance of tutorials available online that offer additional tools and tricks for your specific medium. Watch them, learn, and apply.

9. Practice. Slow down and be patient. Remember, doesn't have to be perfect.

10. Just color. And HAVE FUN!

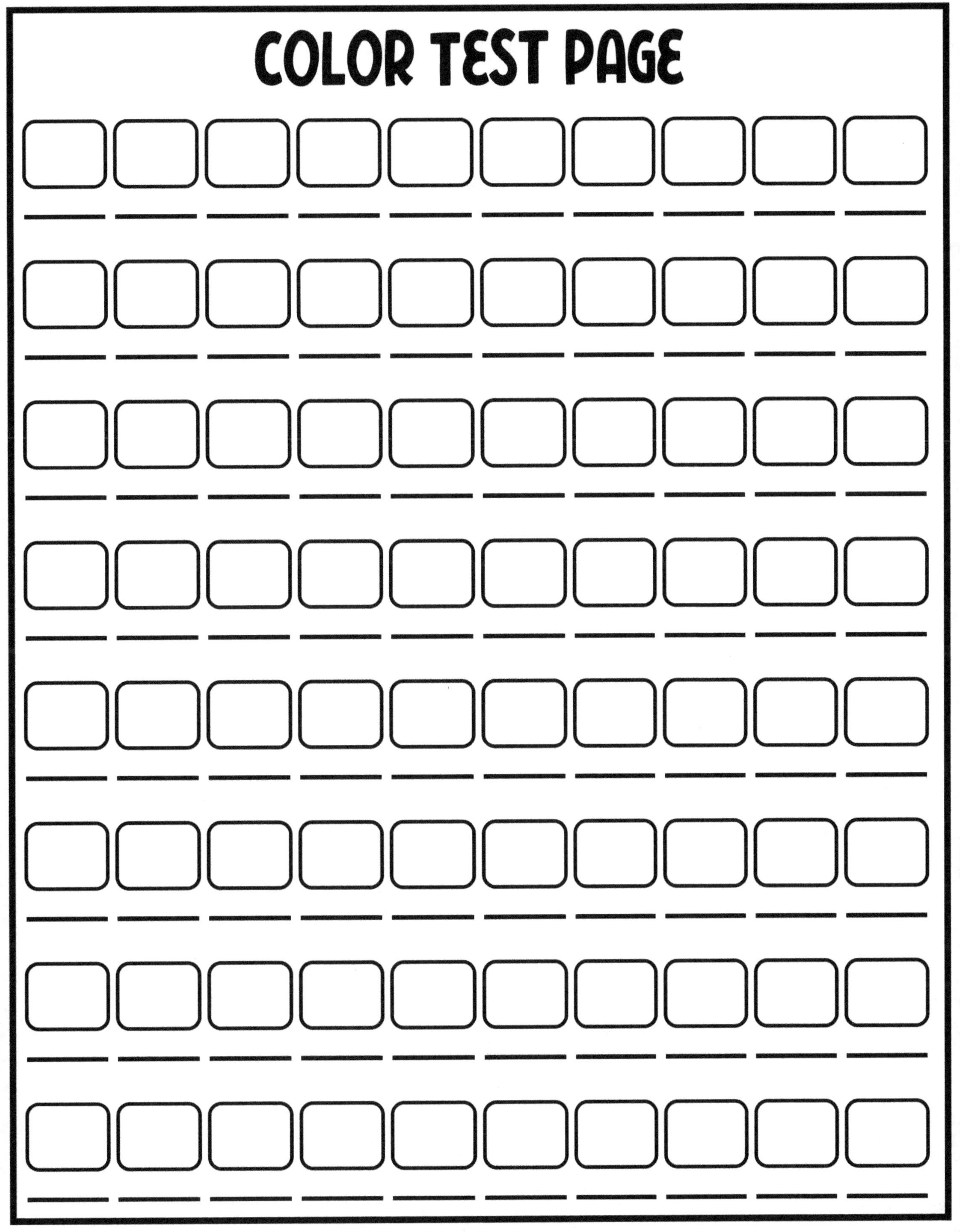
COLOR TEST PAGE

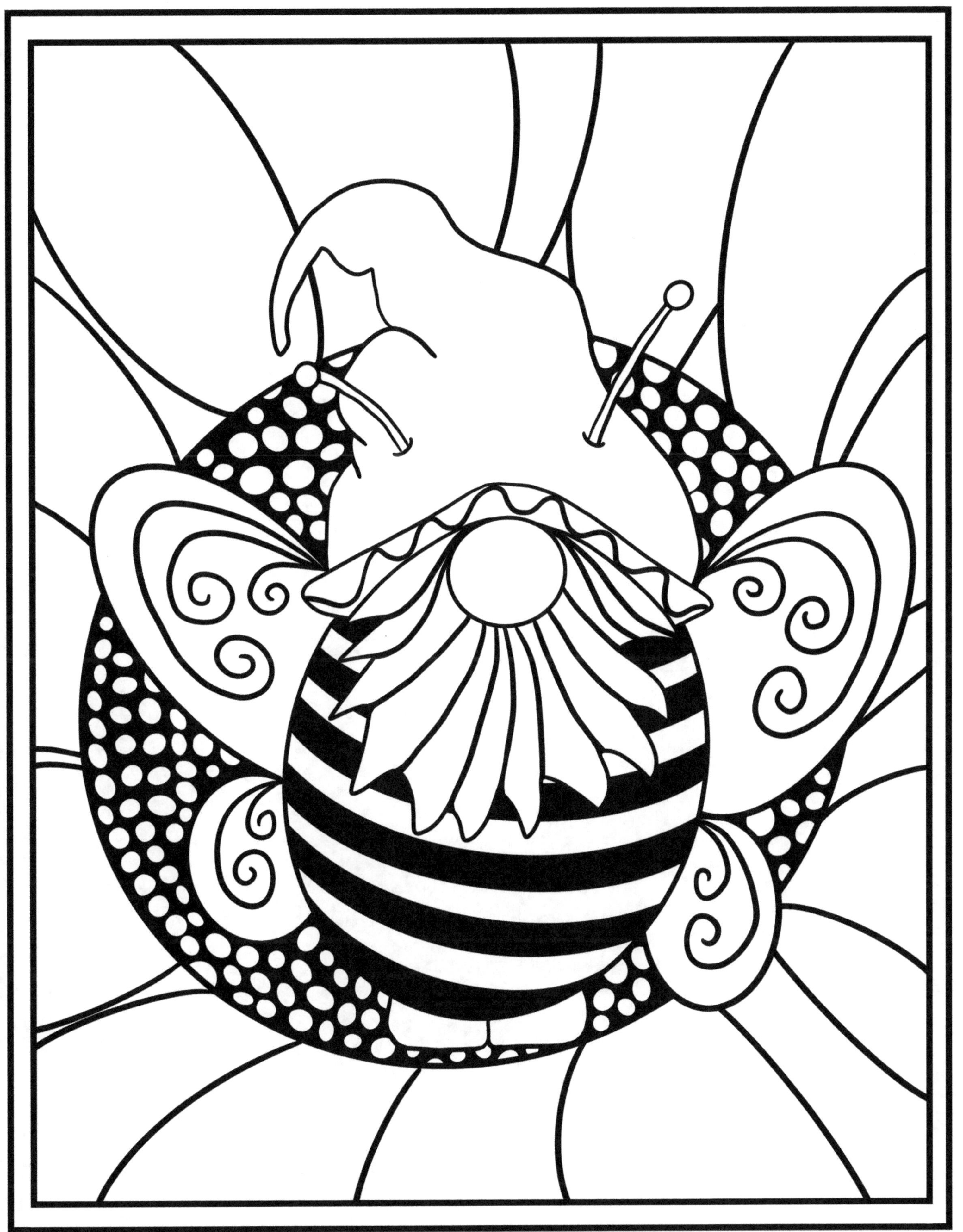

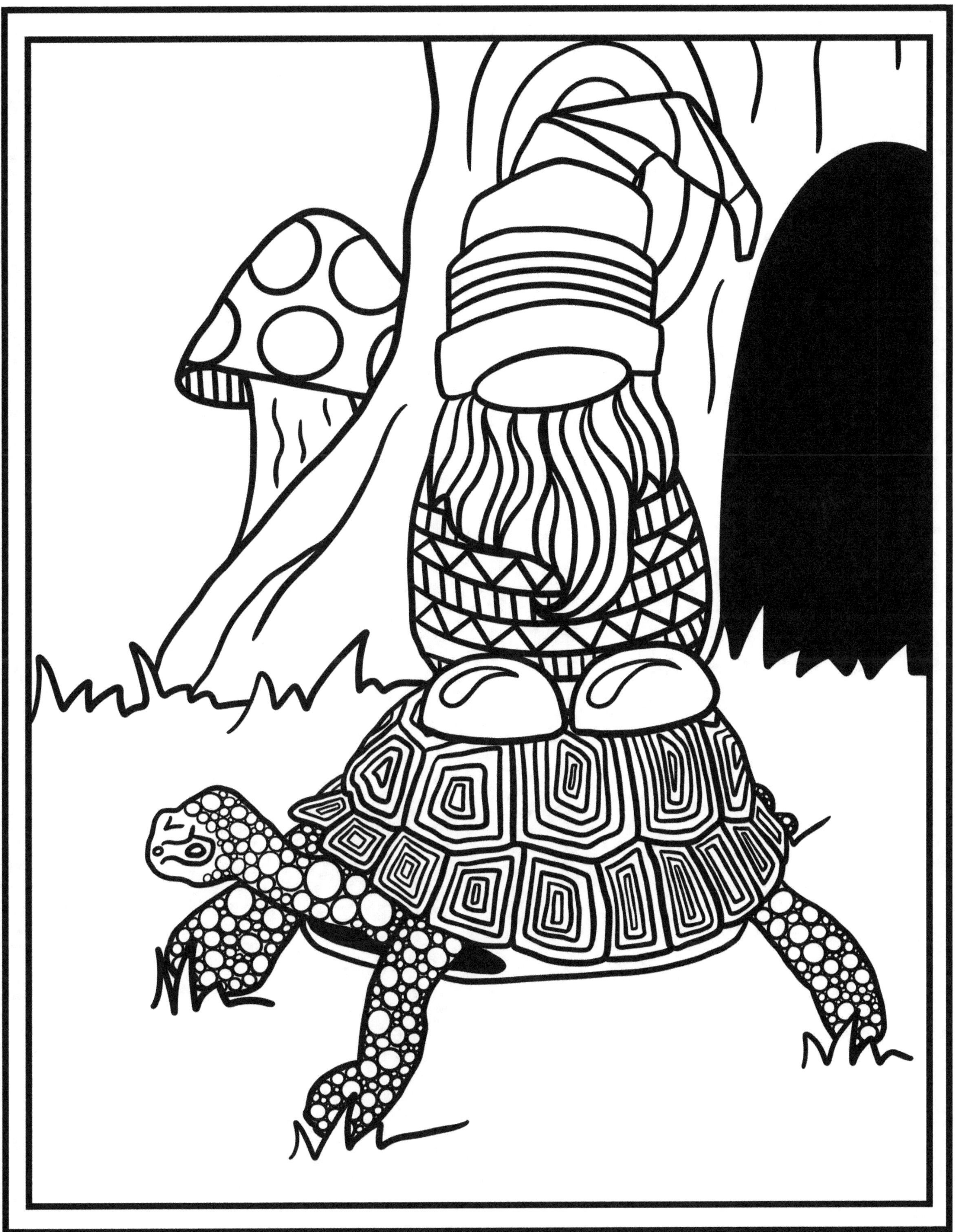

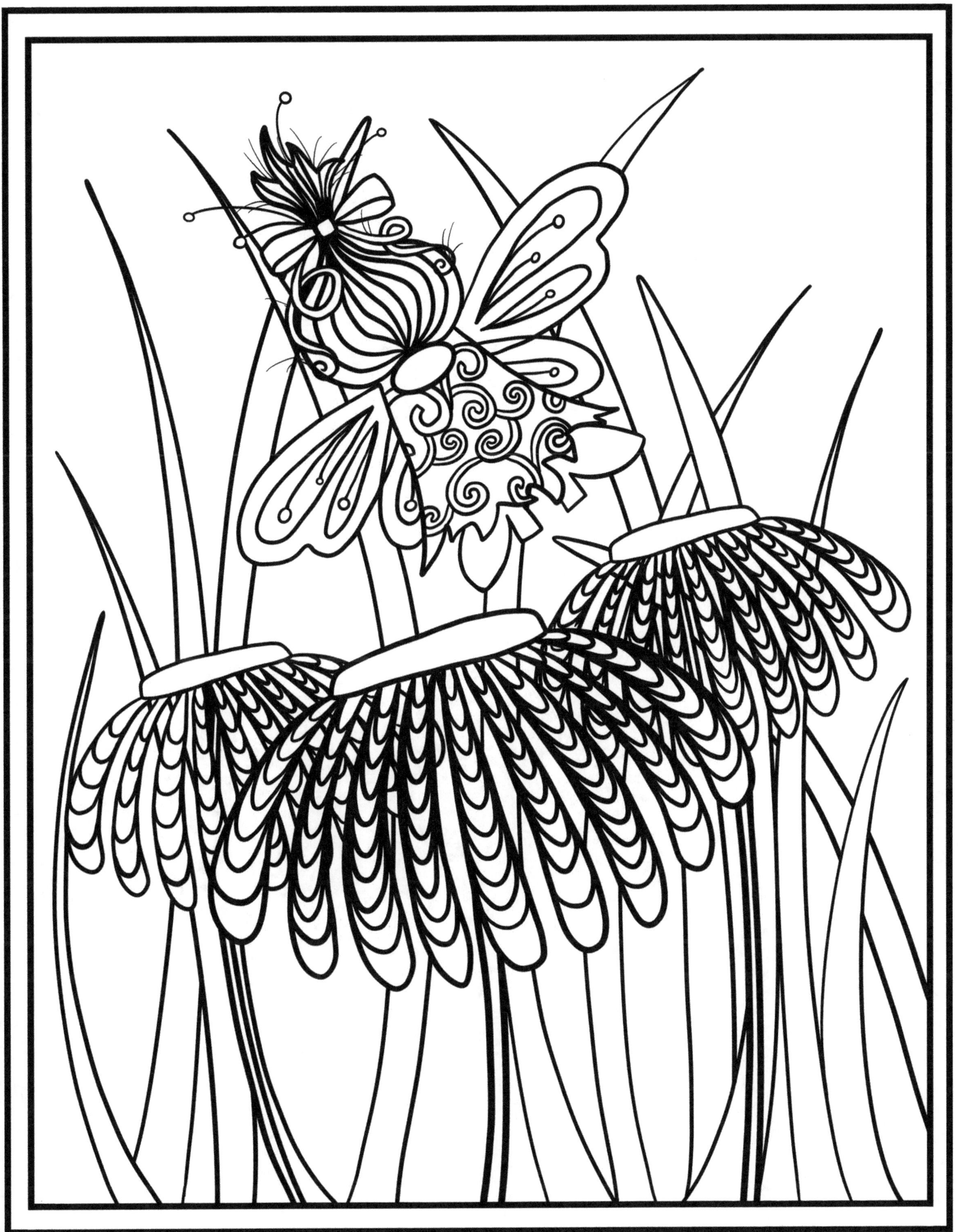

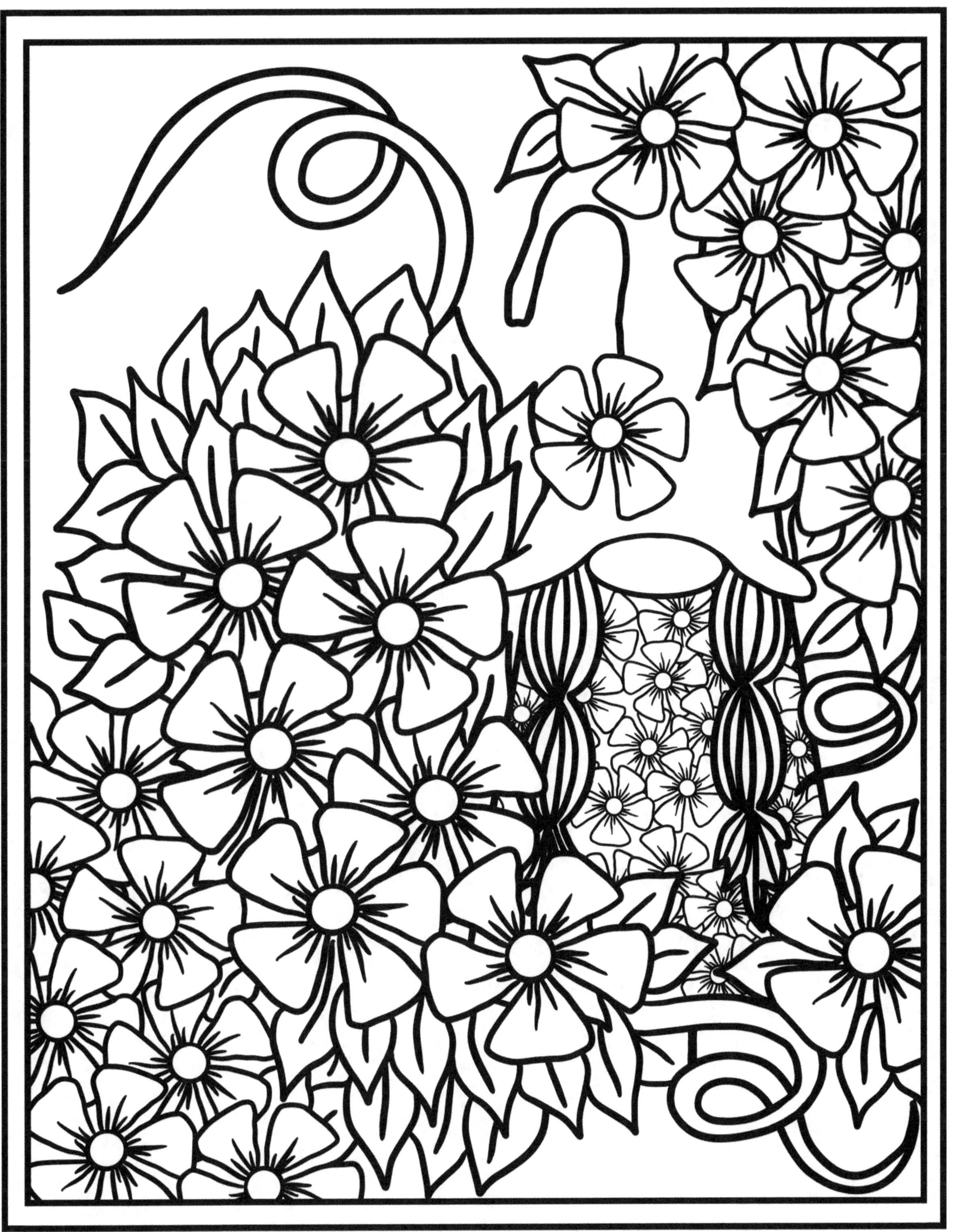

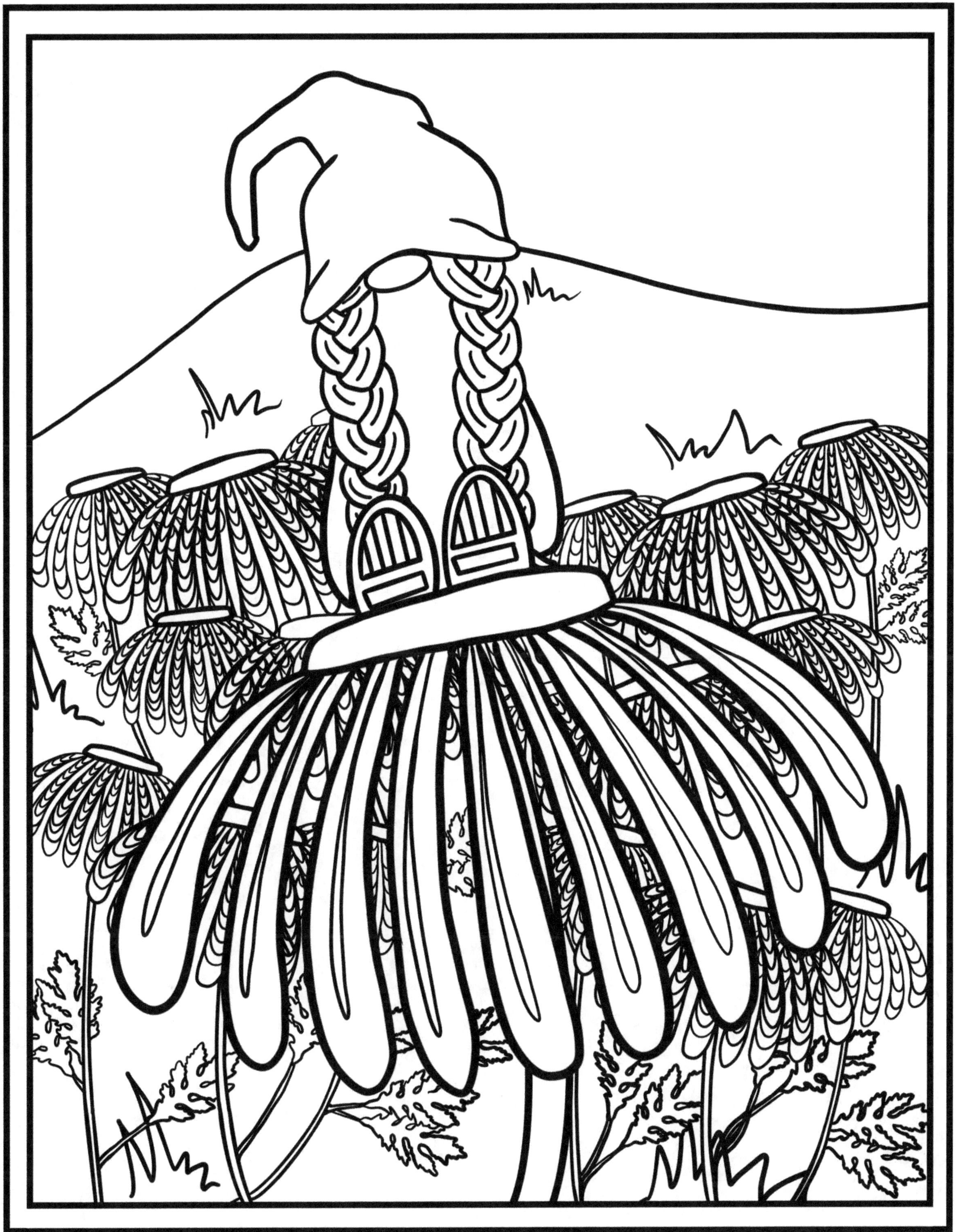

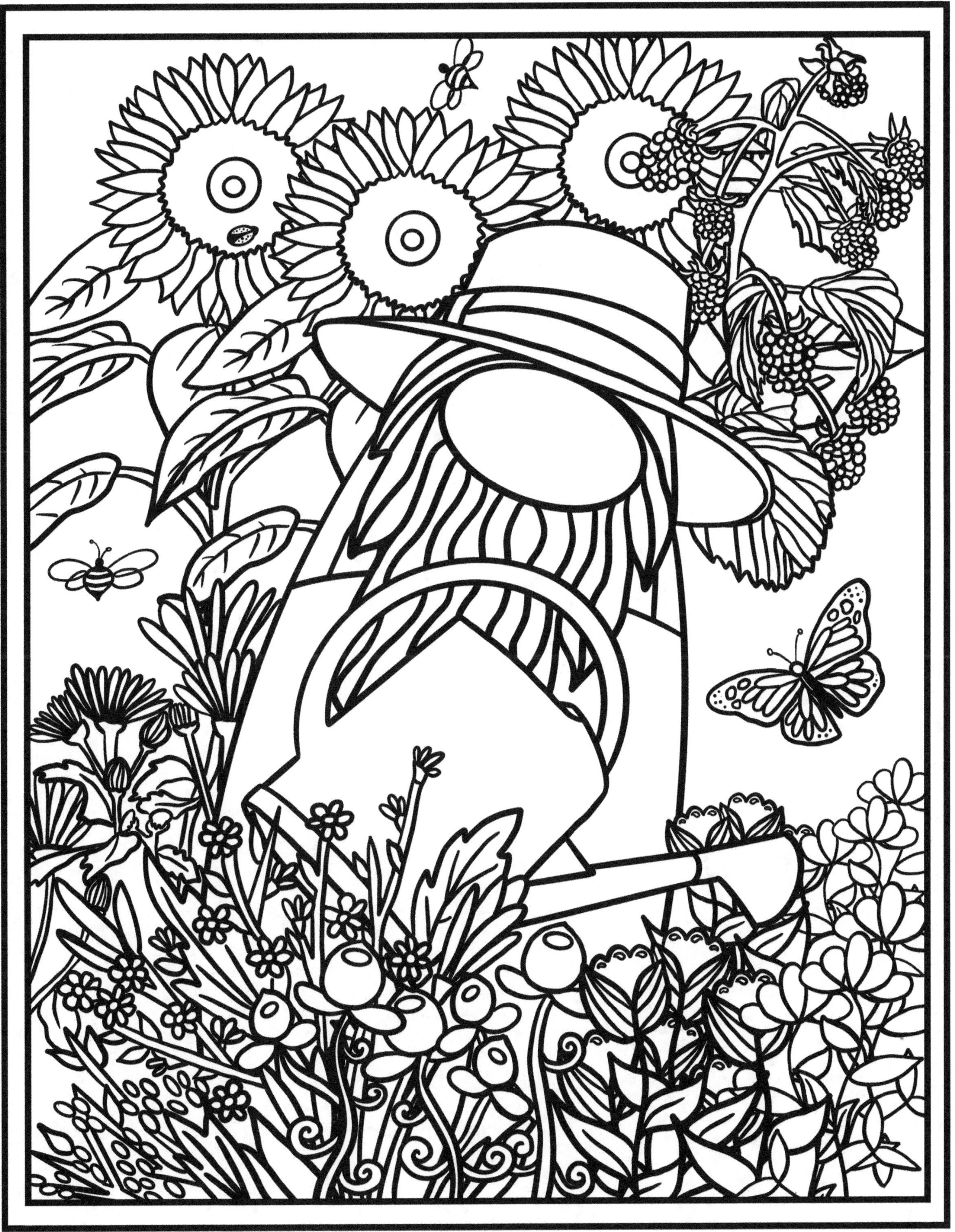

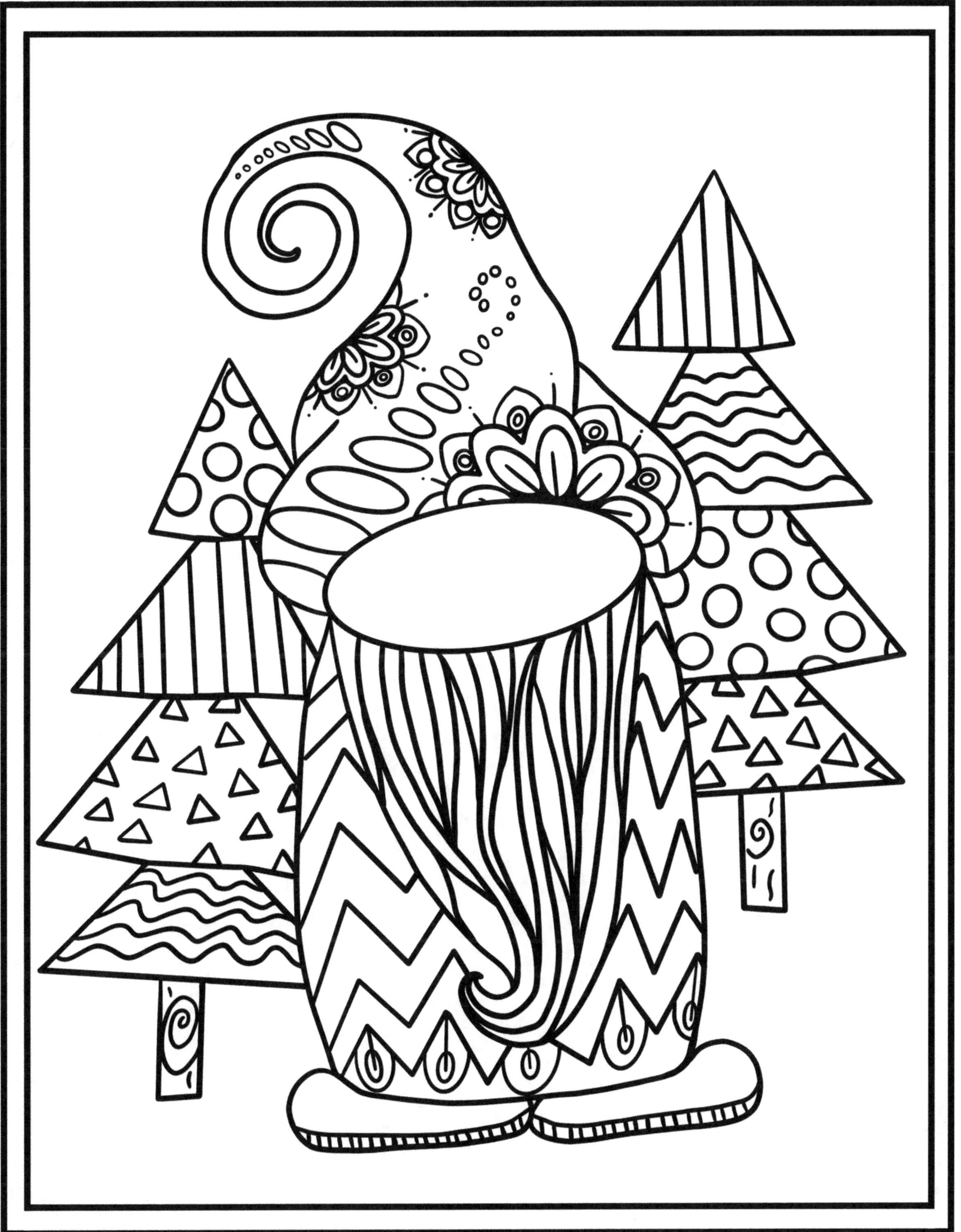

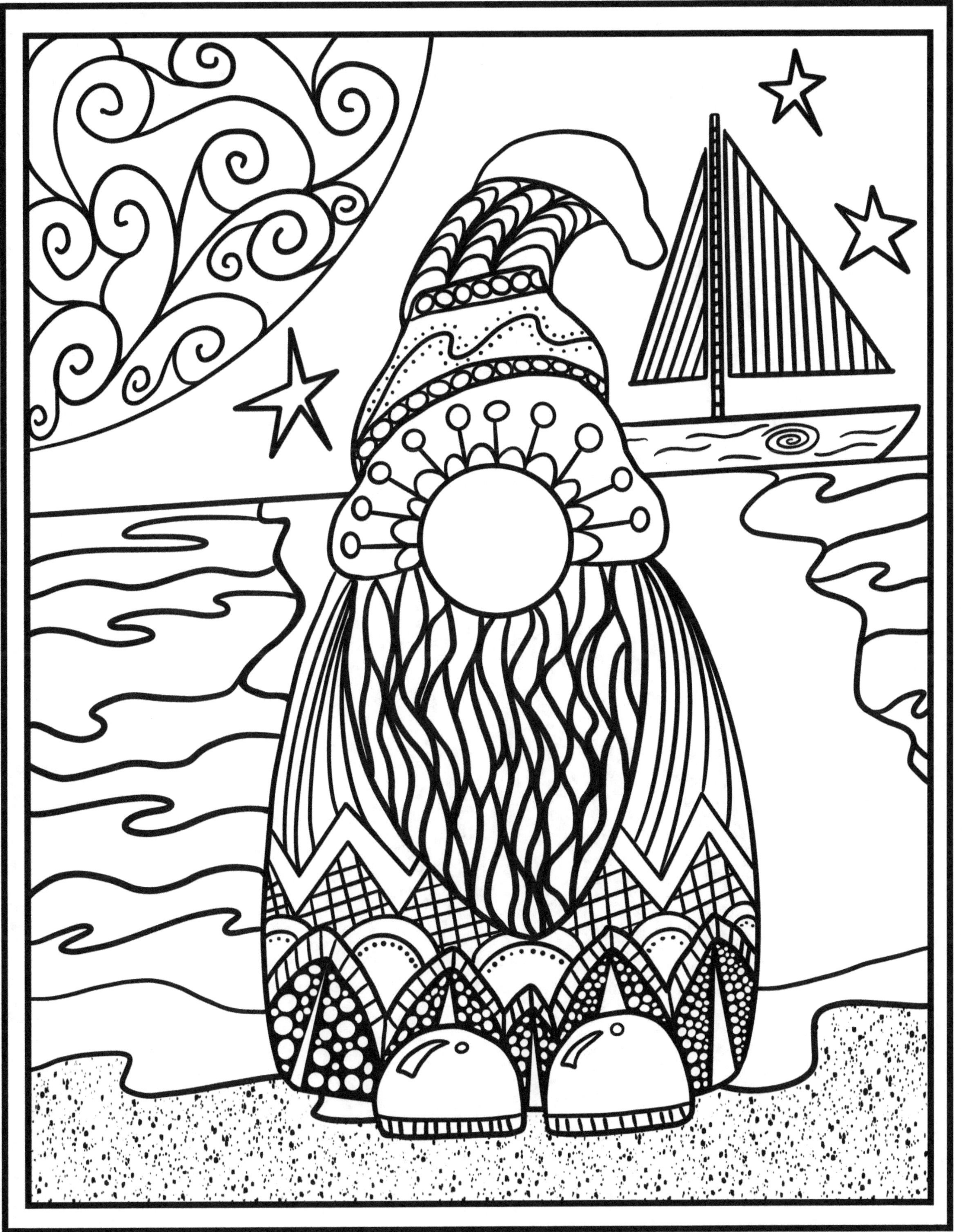

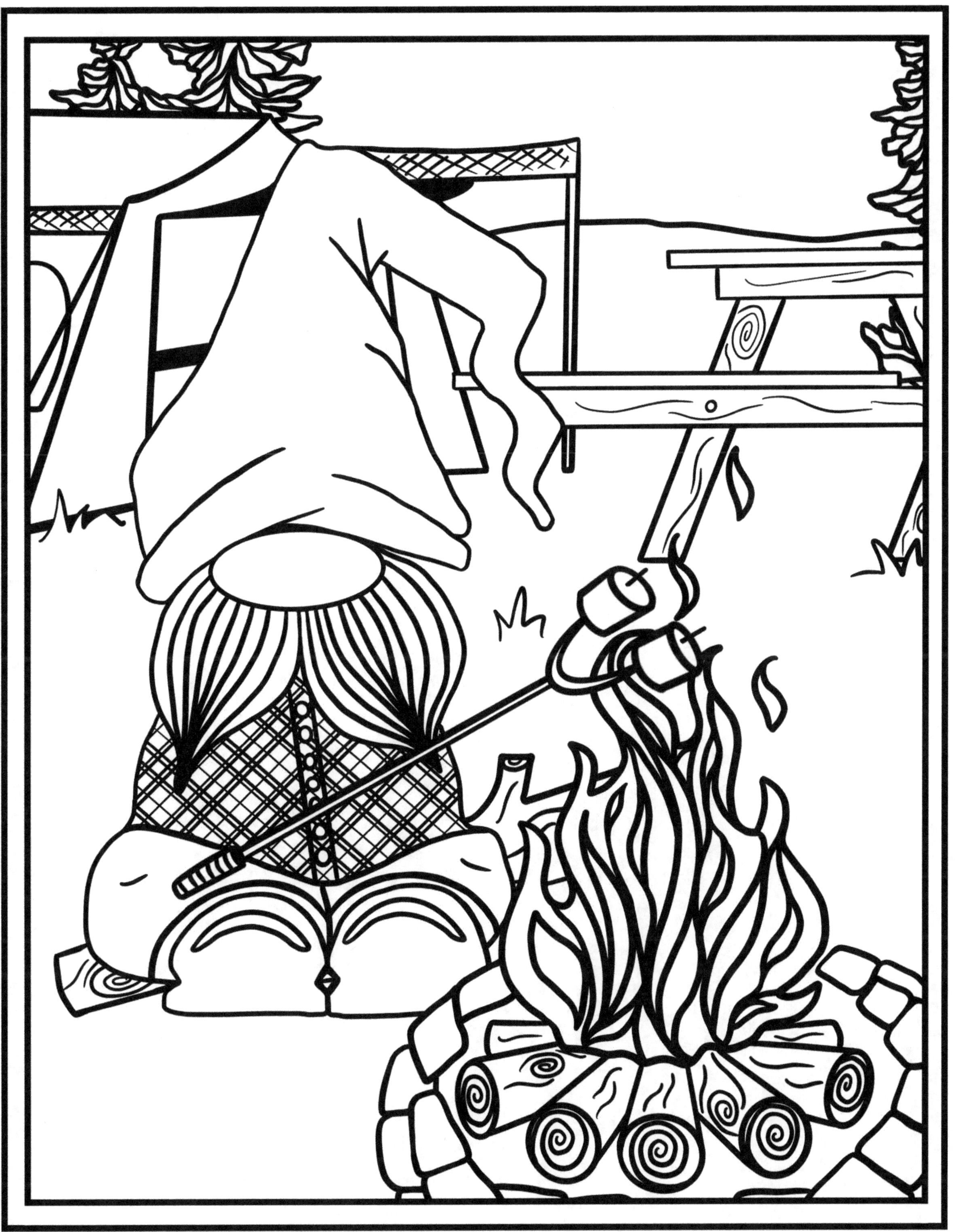

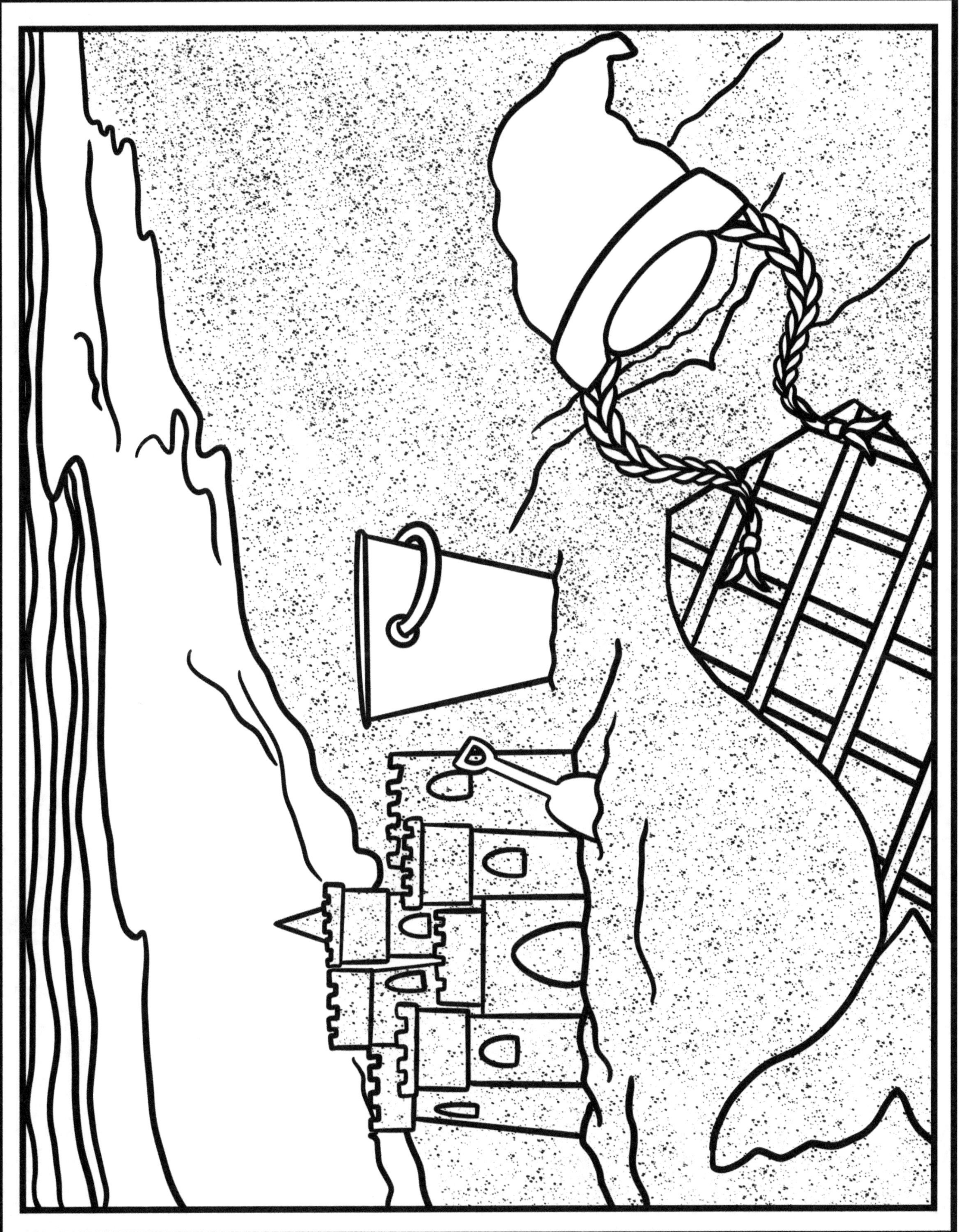

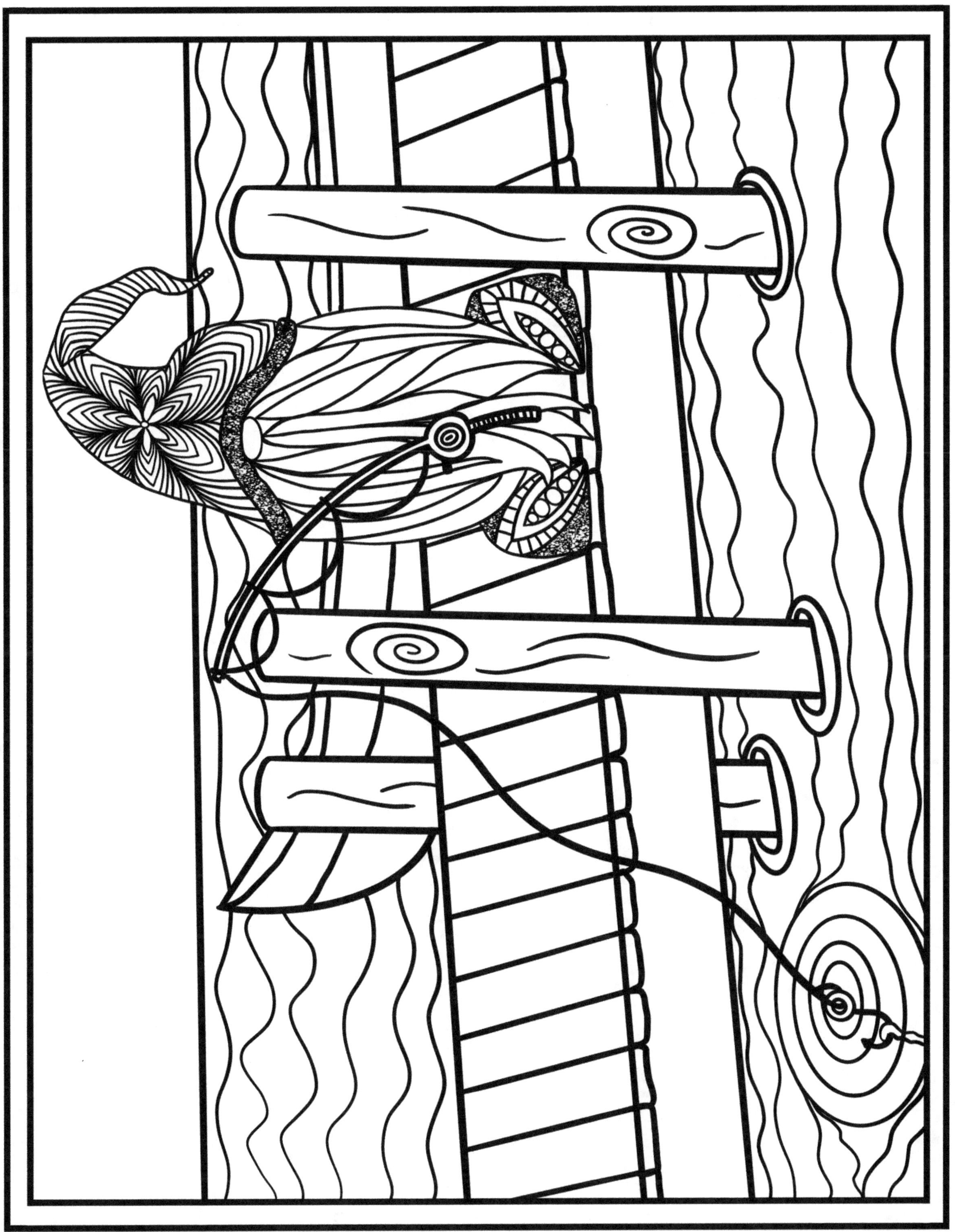

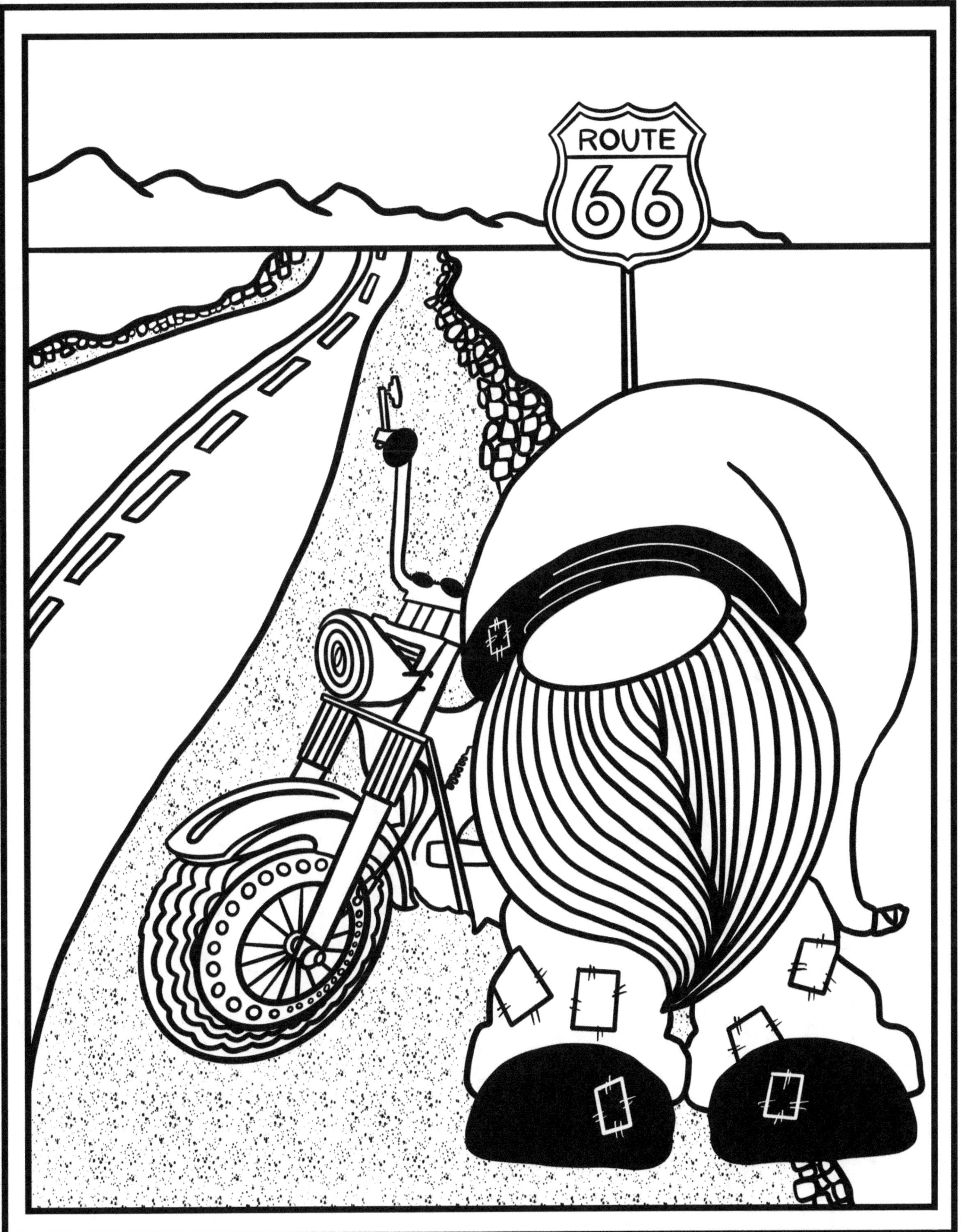
ROUTE
66

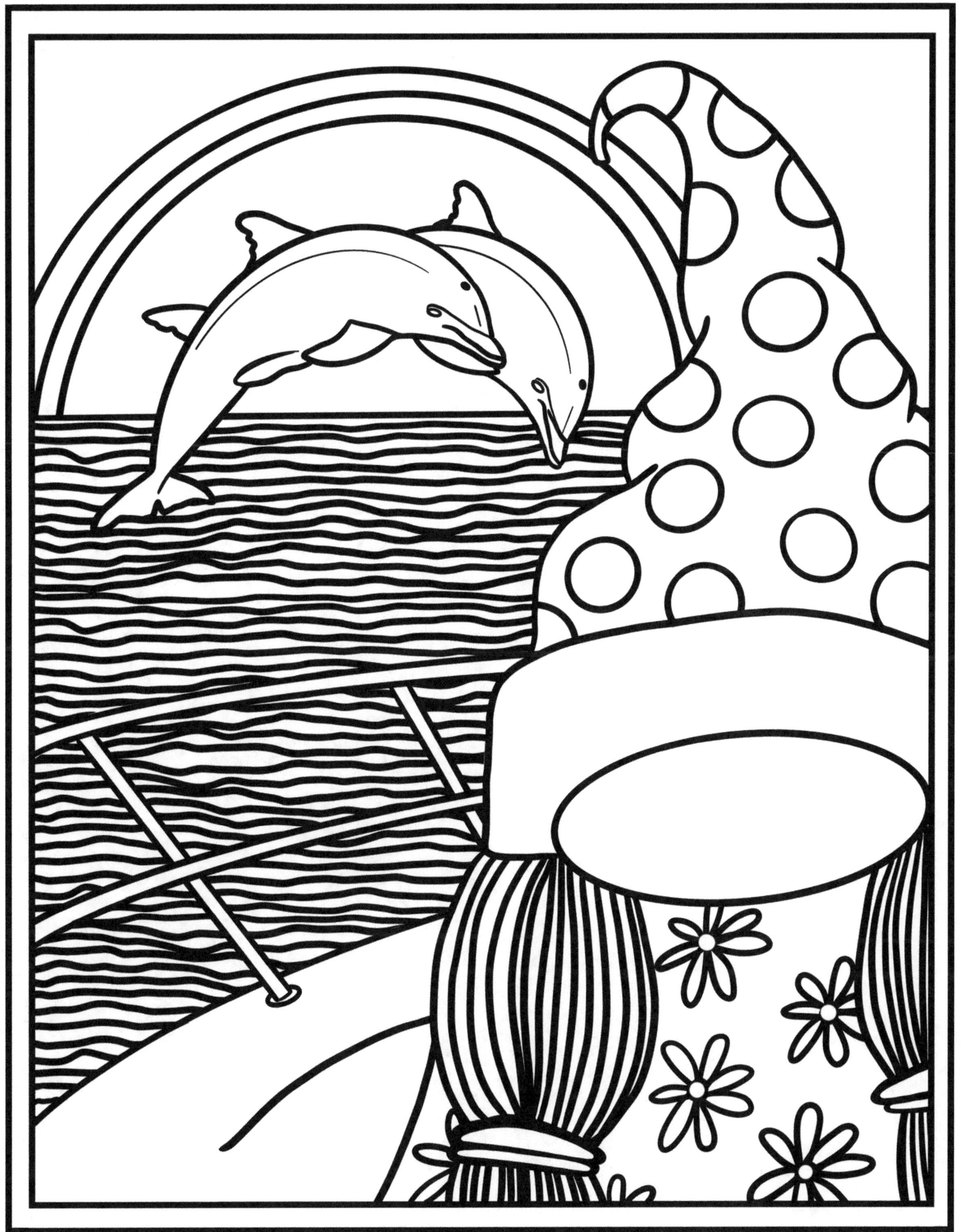

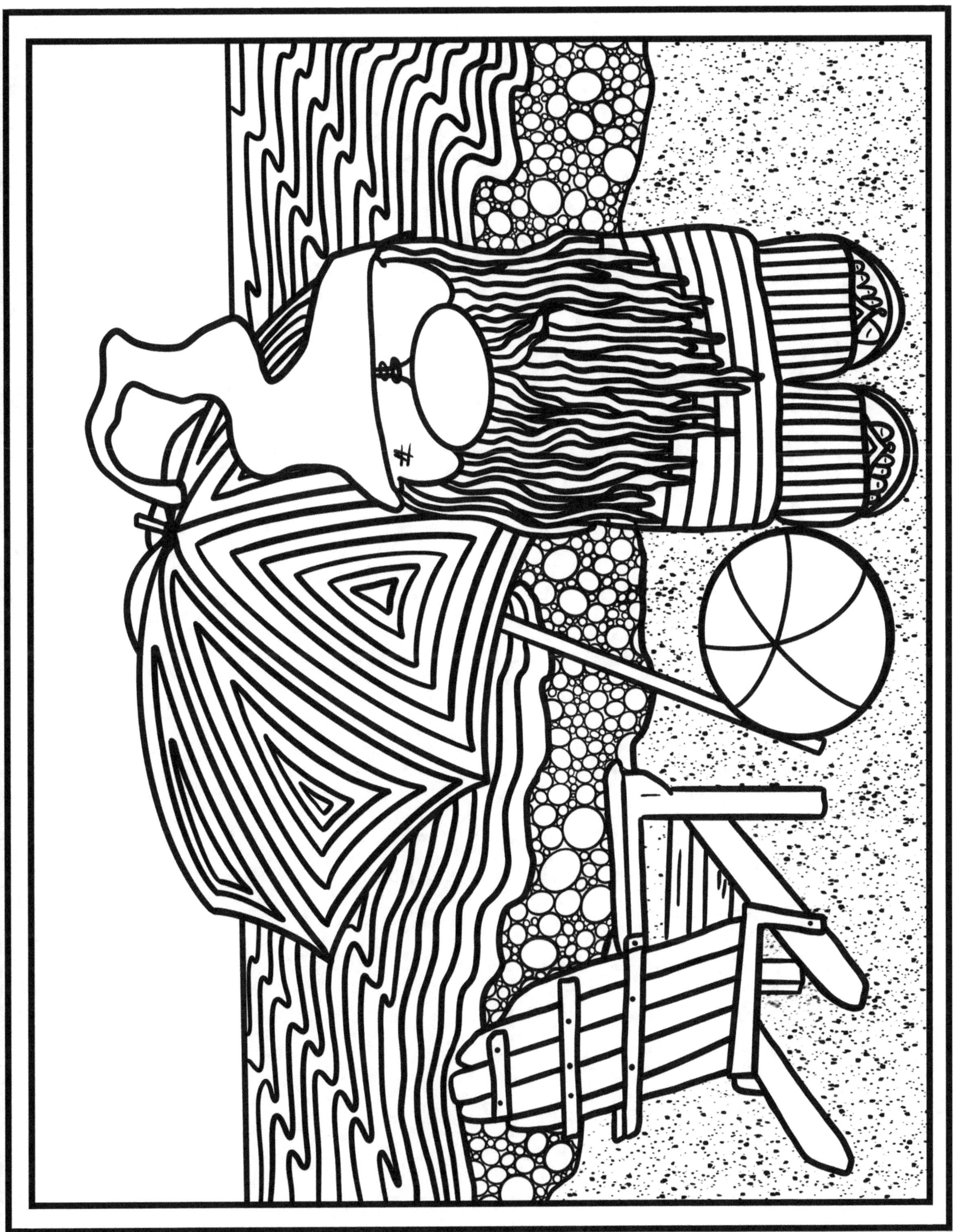

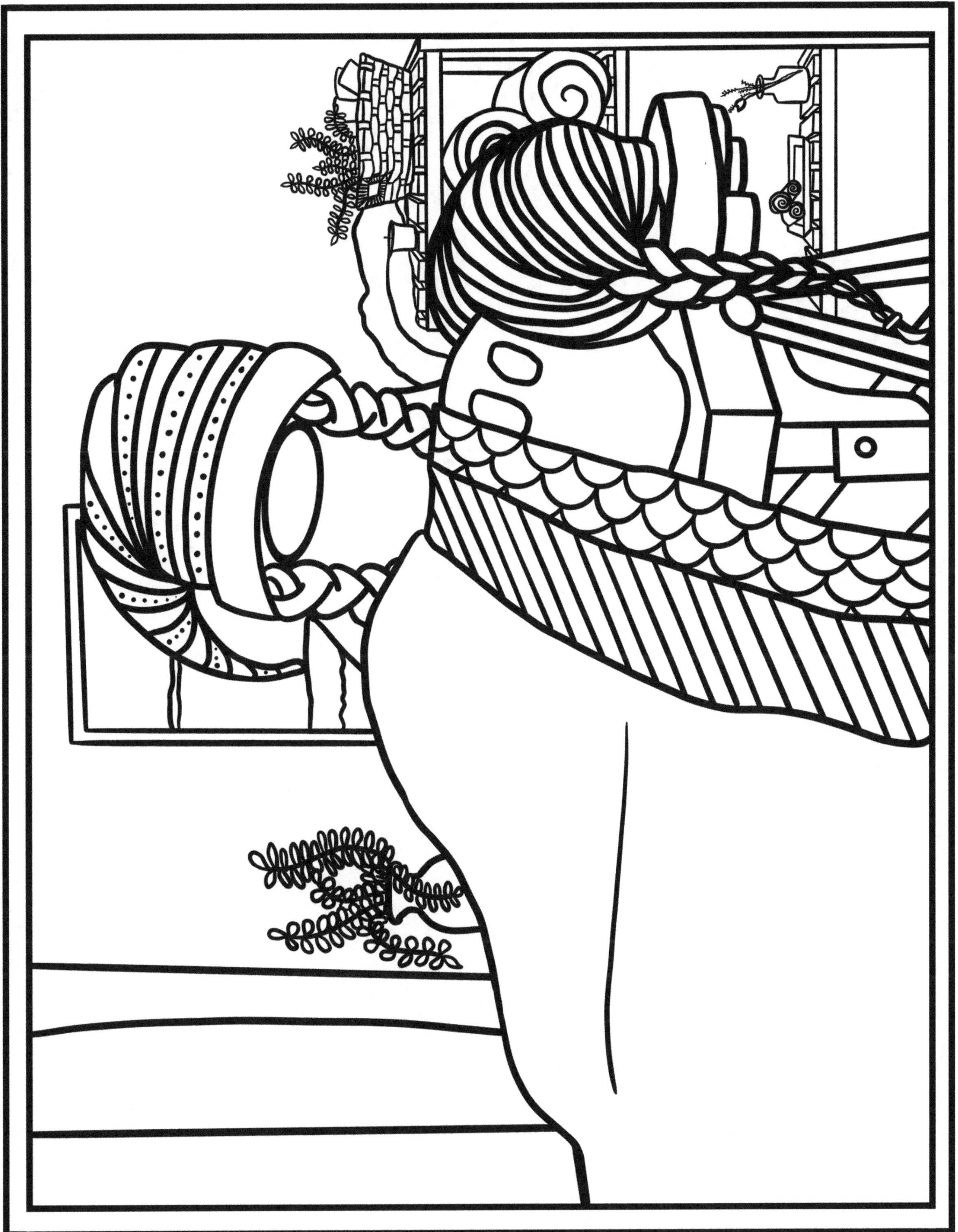

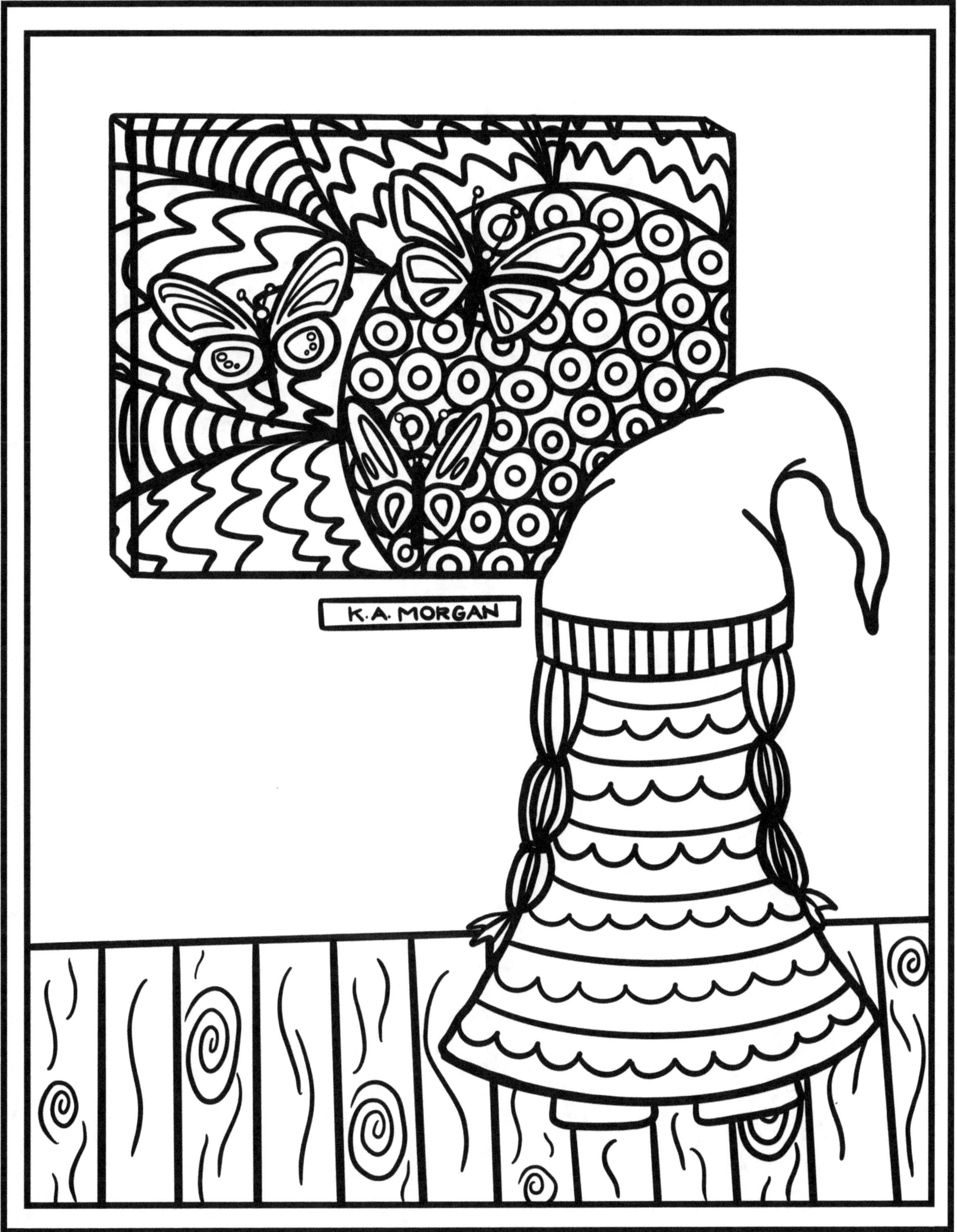
K.A. MORGAN

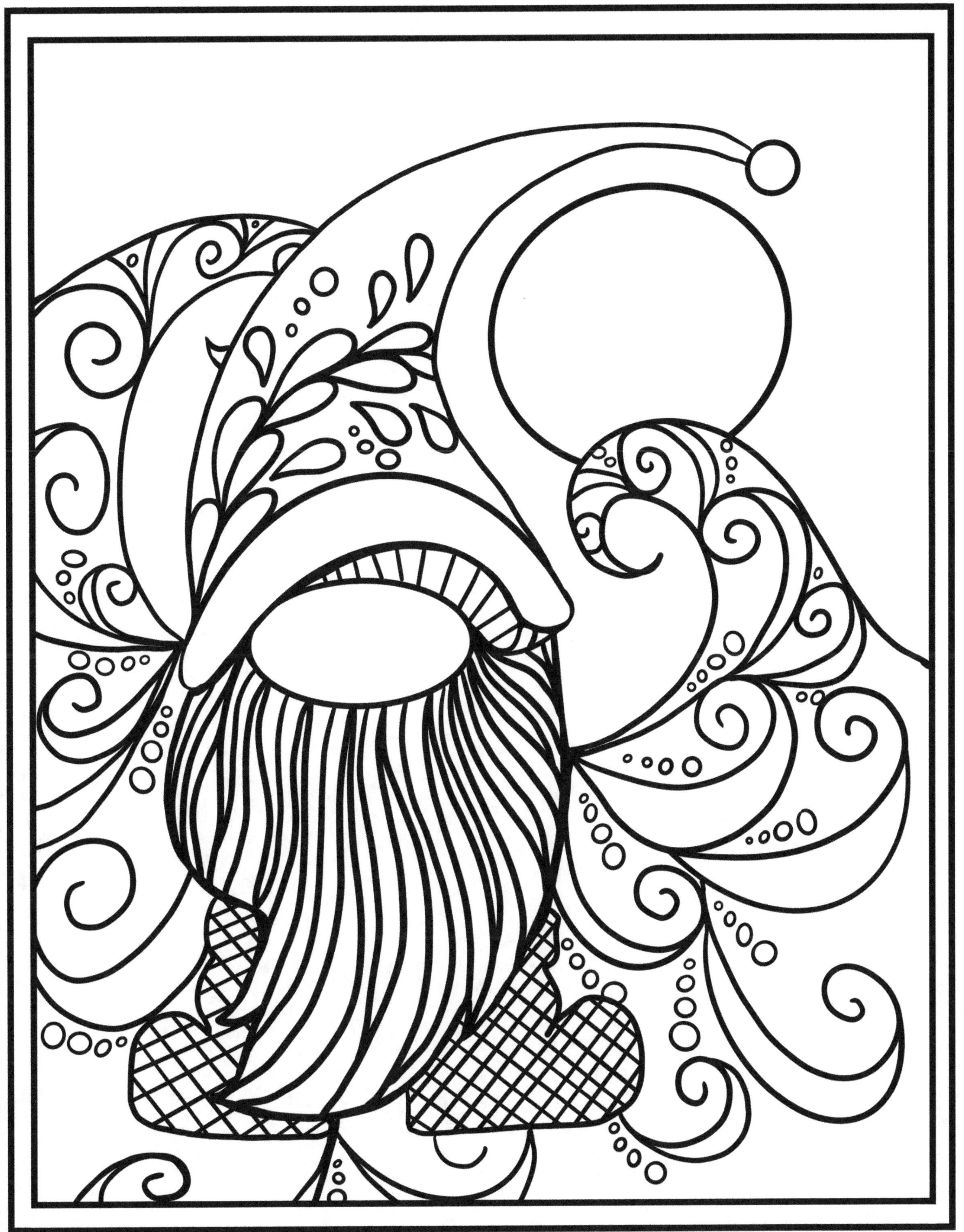

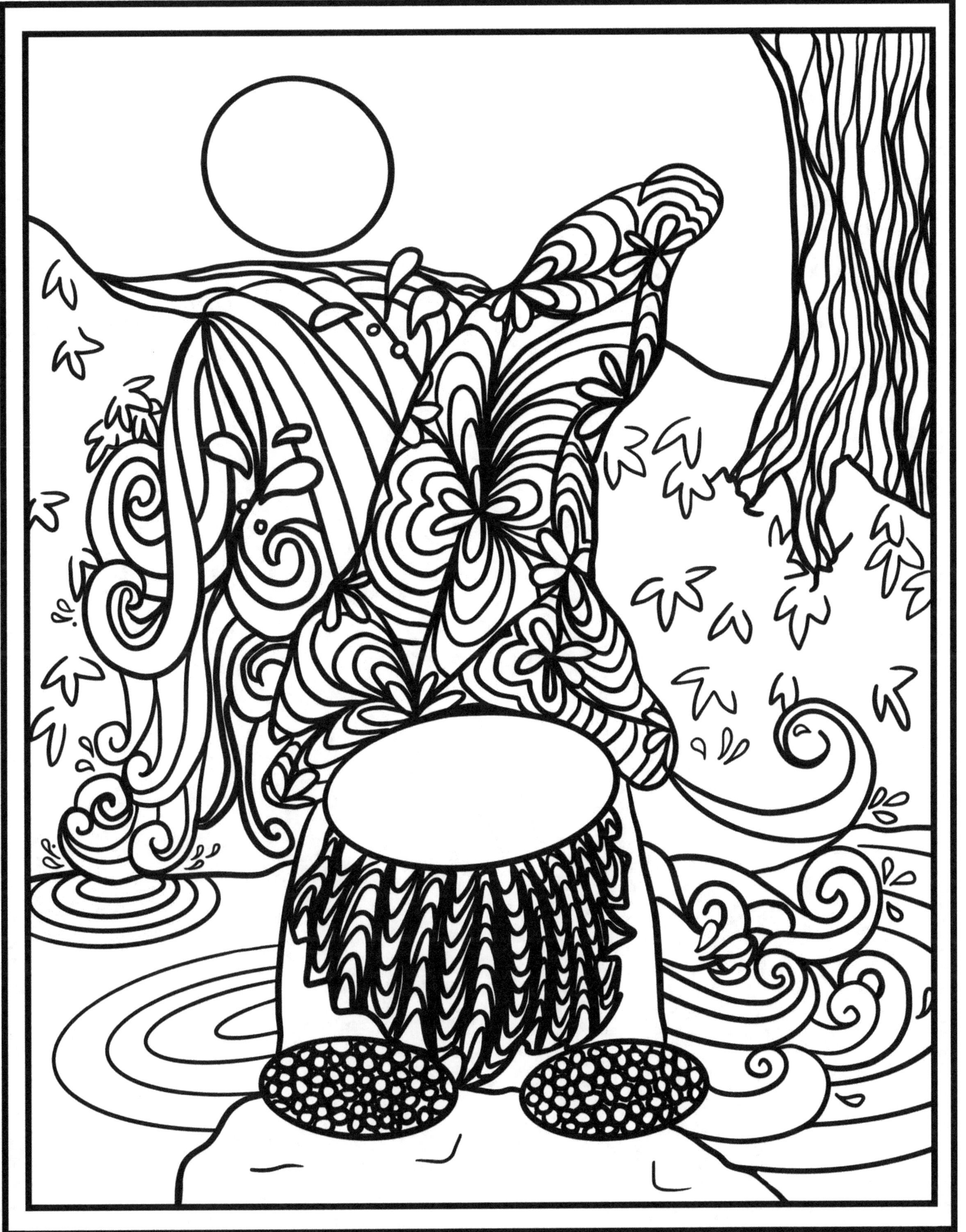

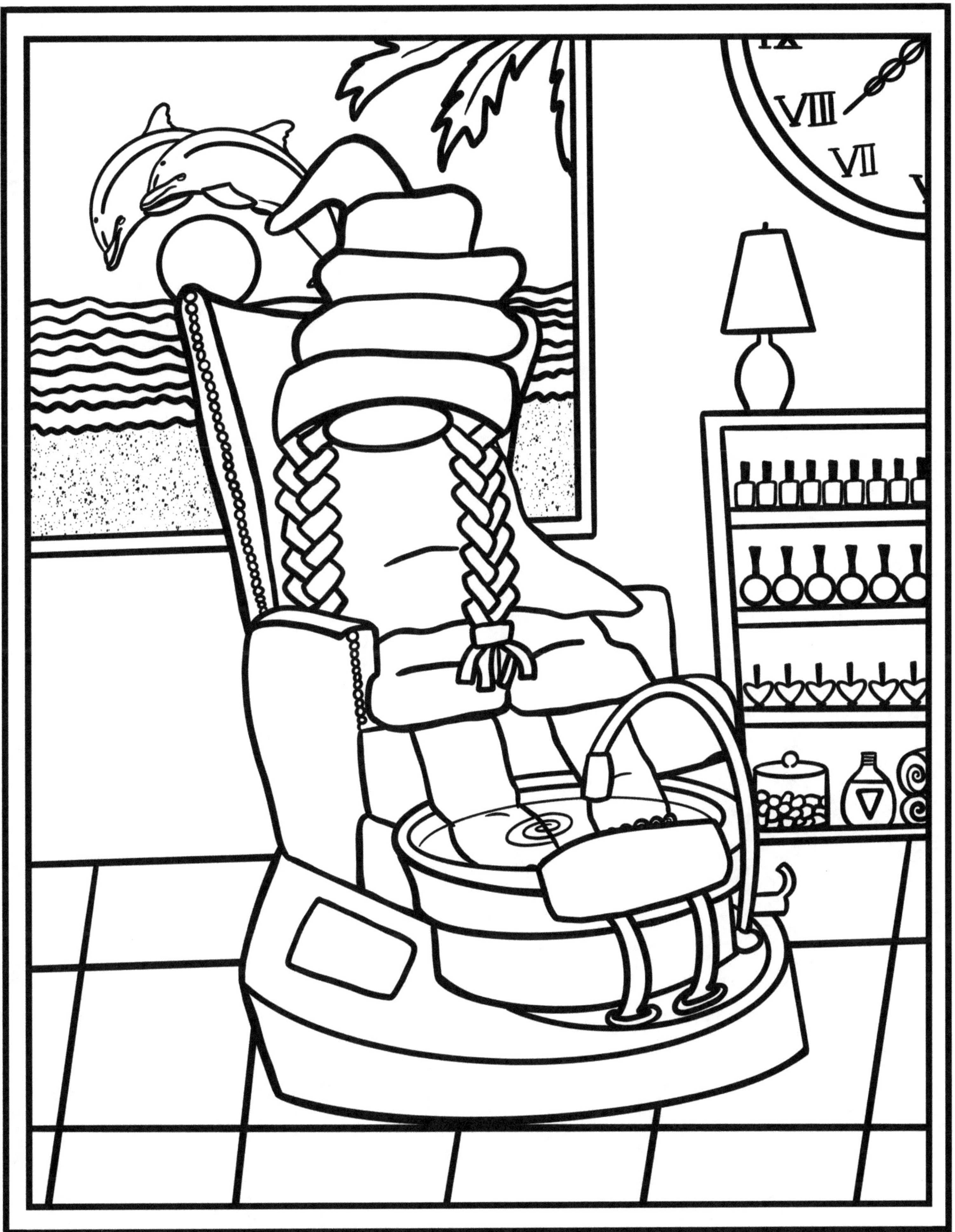
VIII
VII

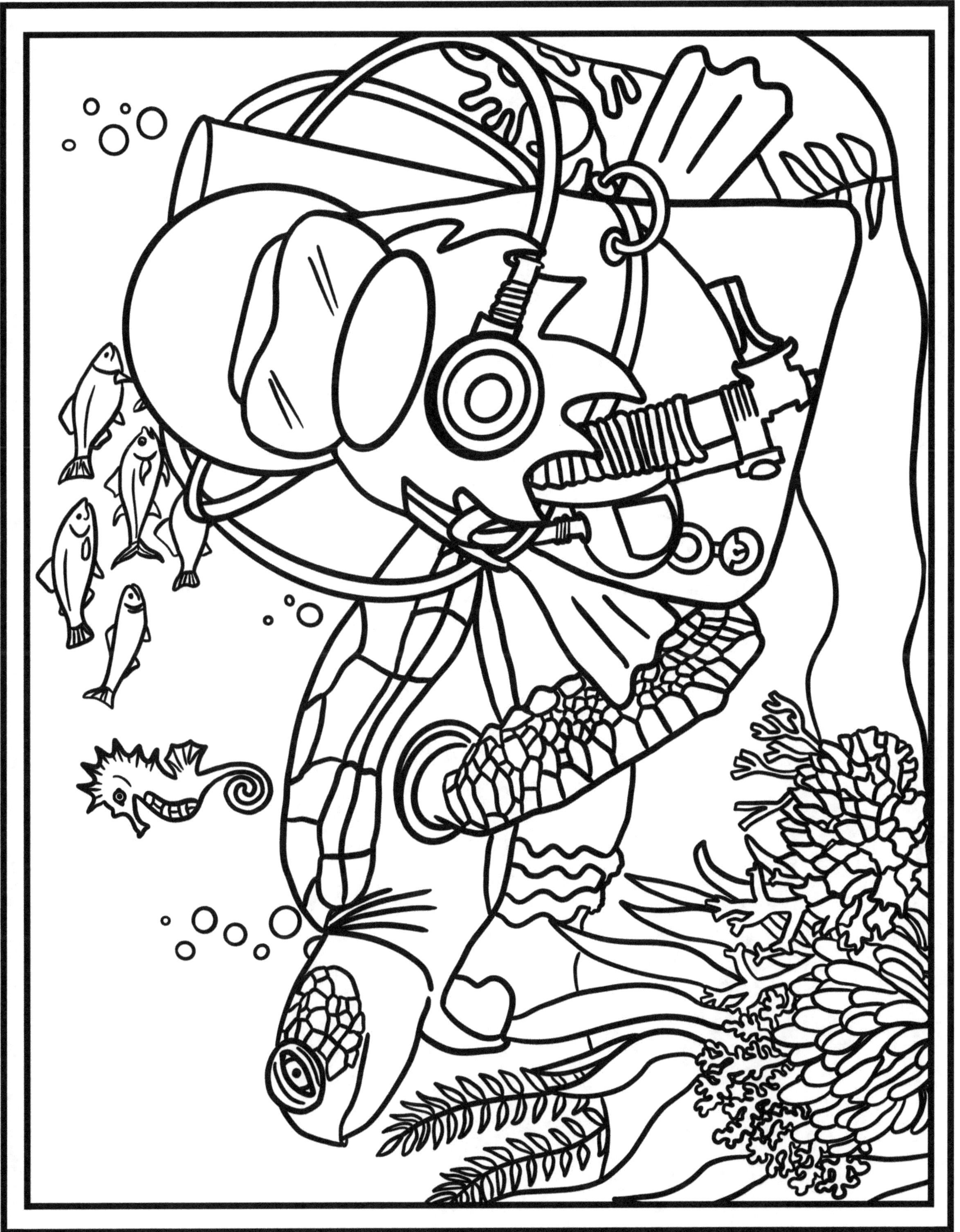

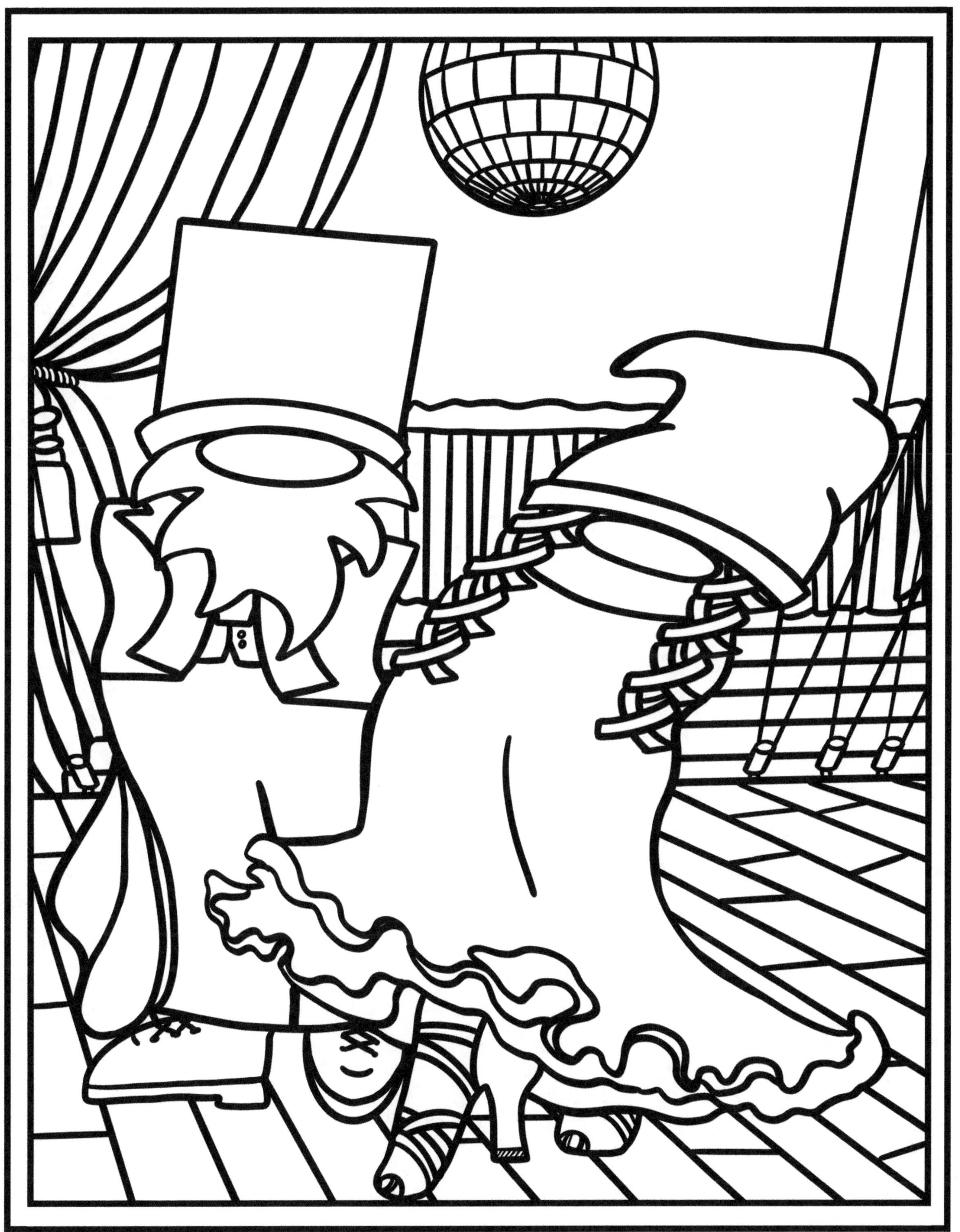

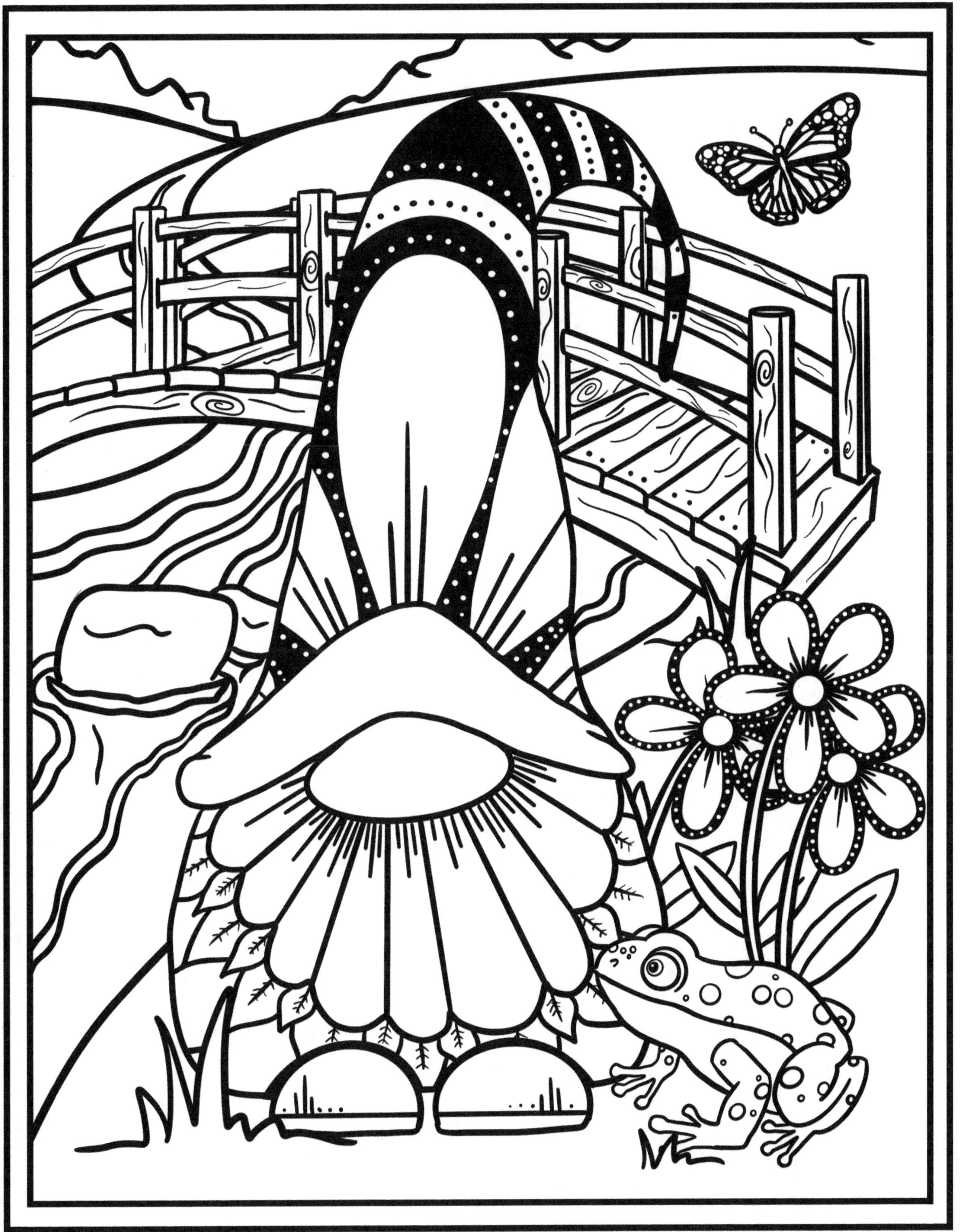

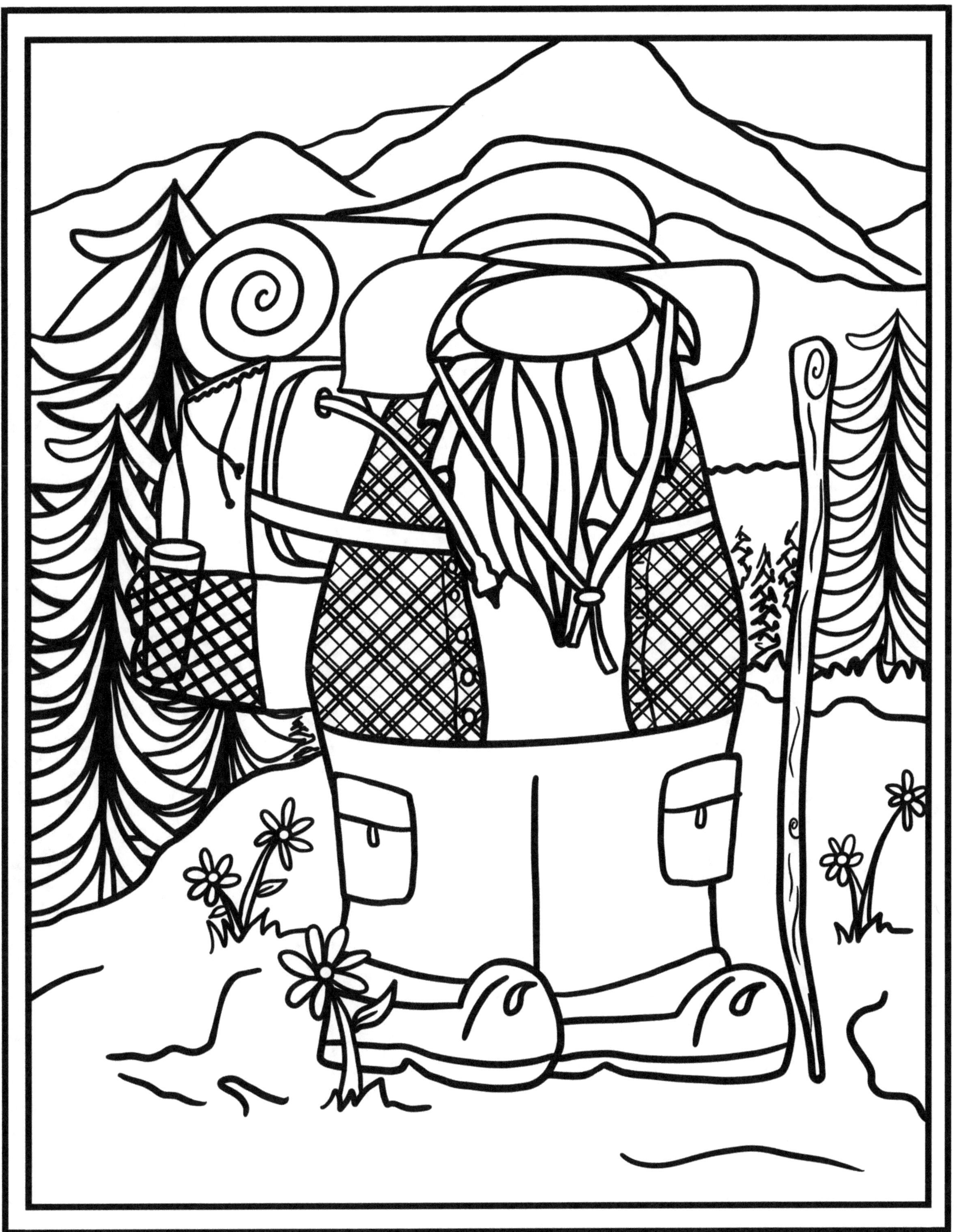

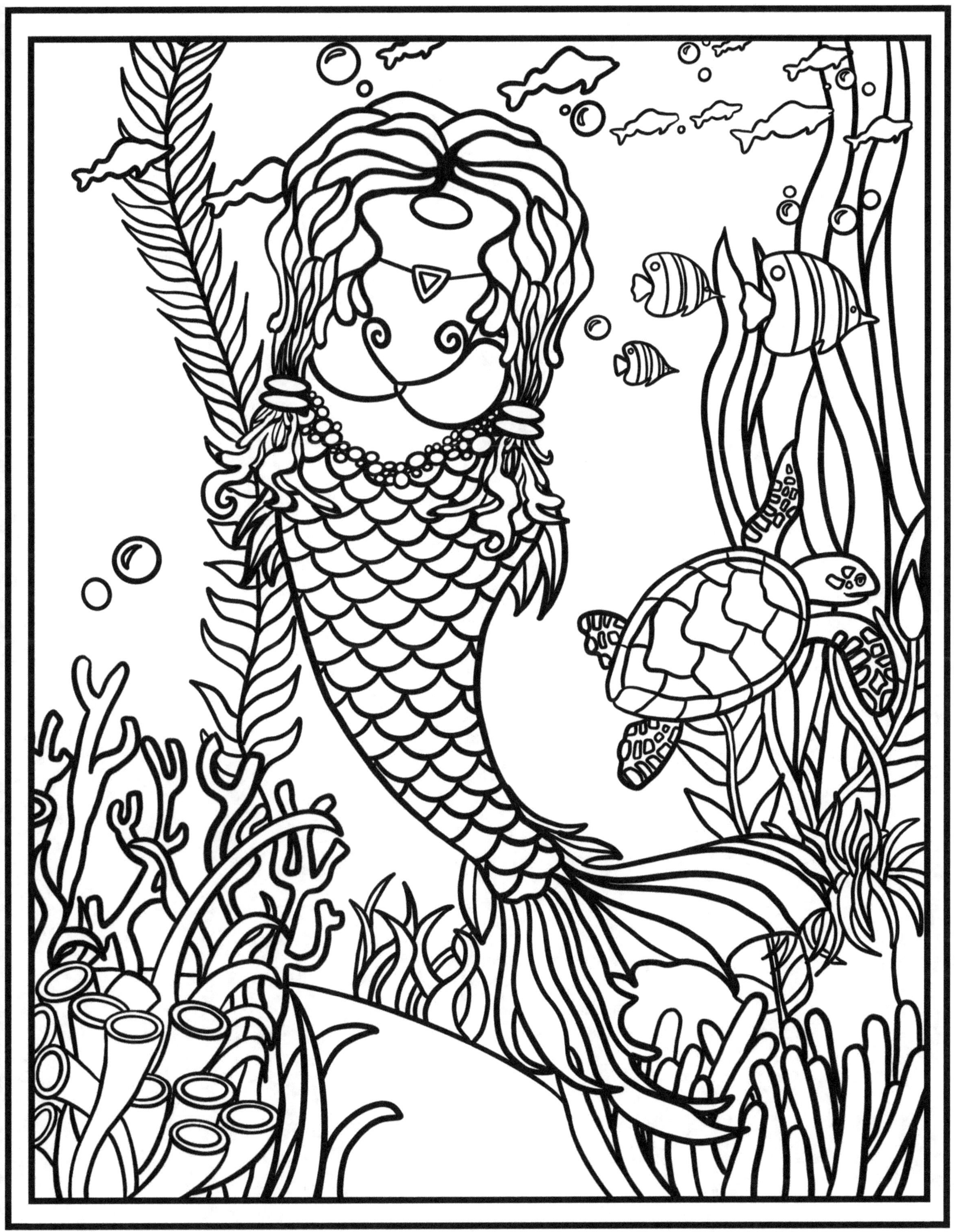

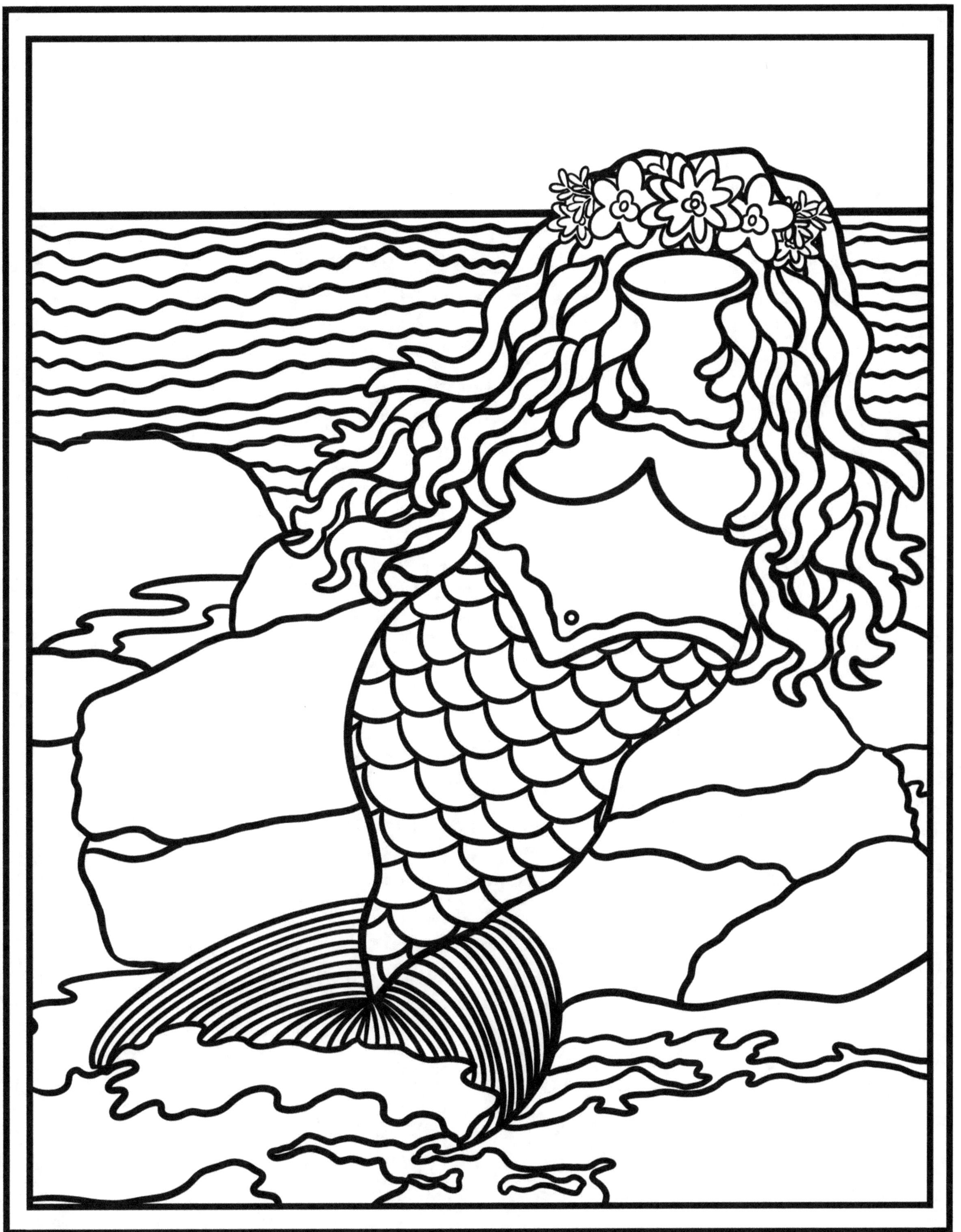

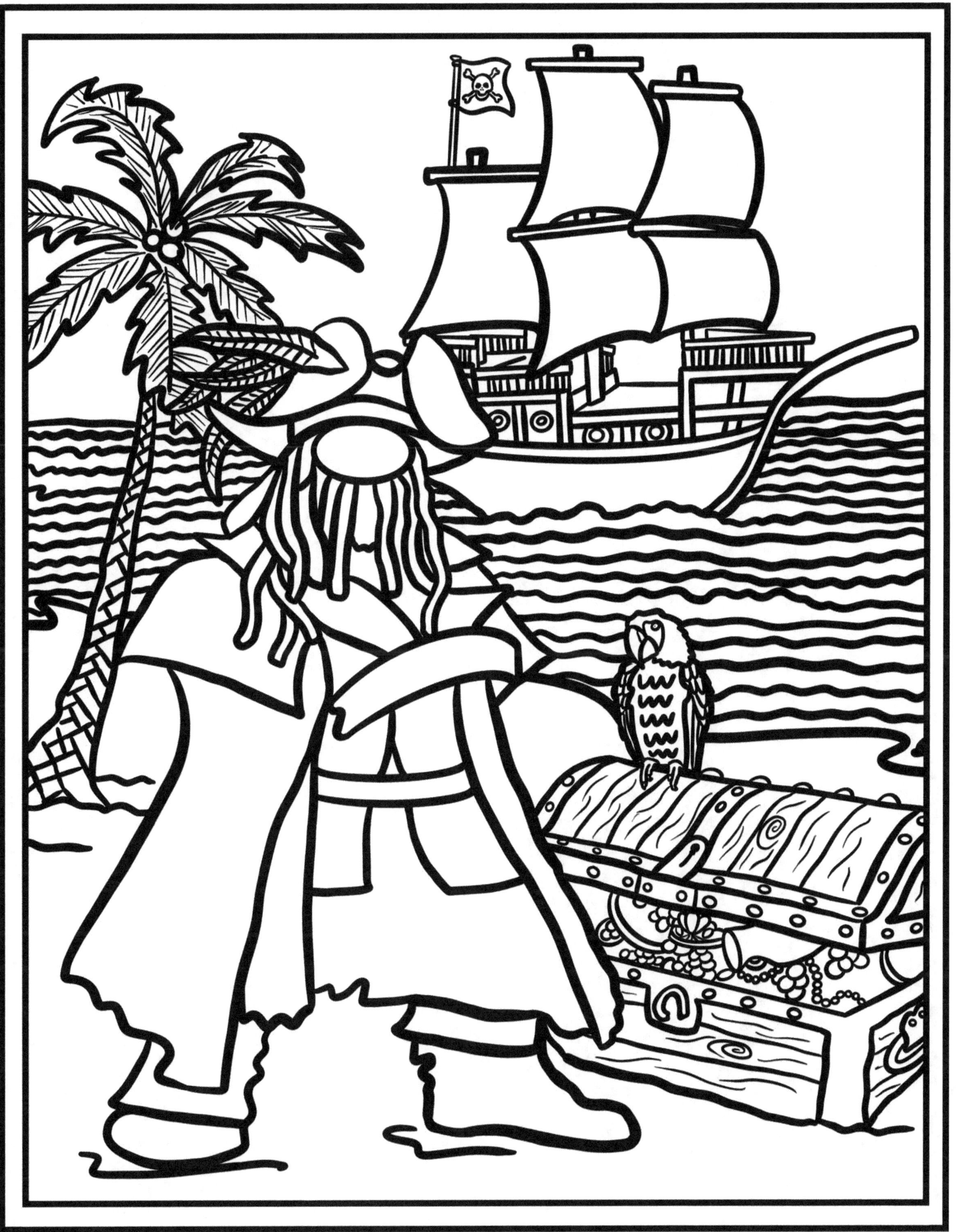

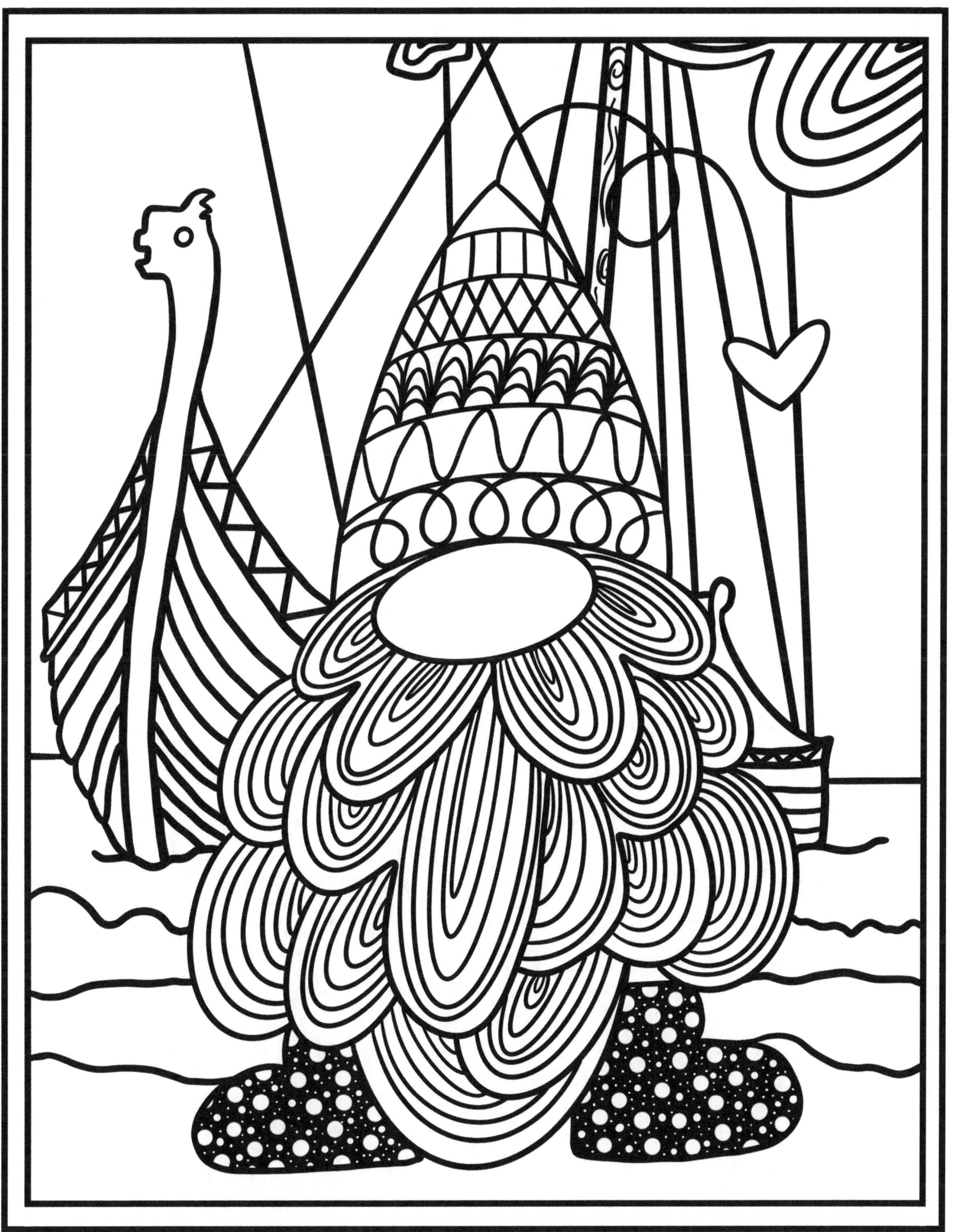

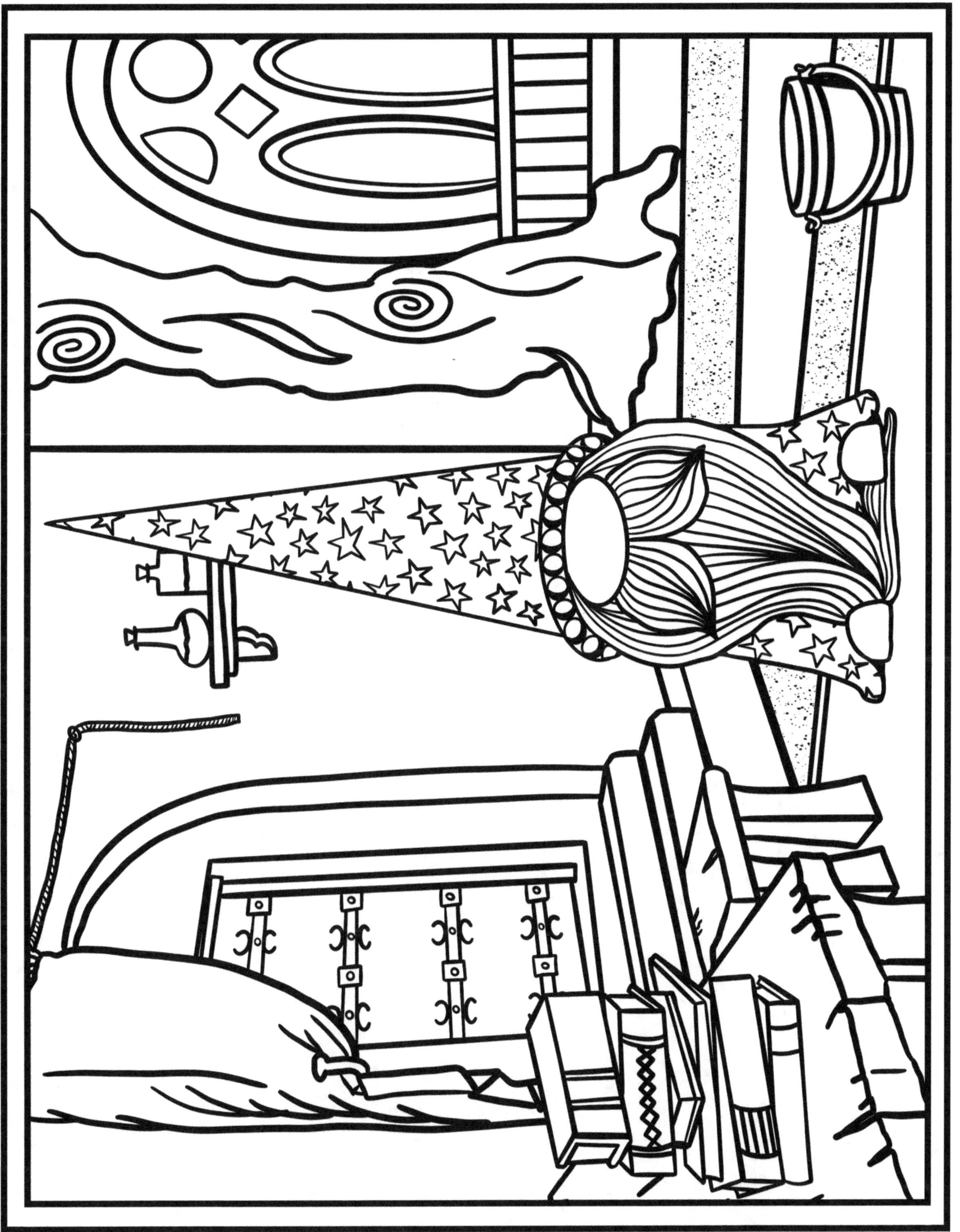

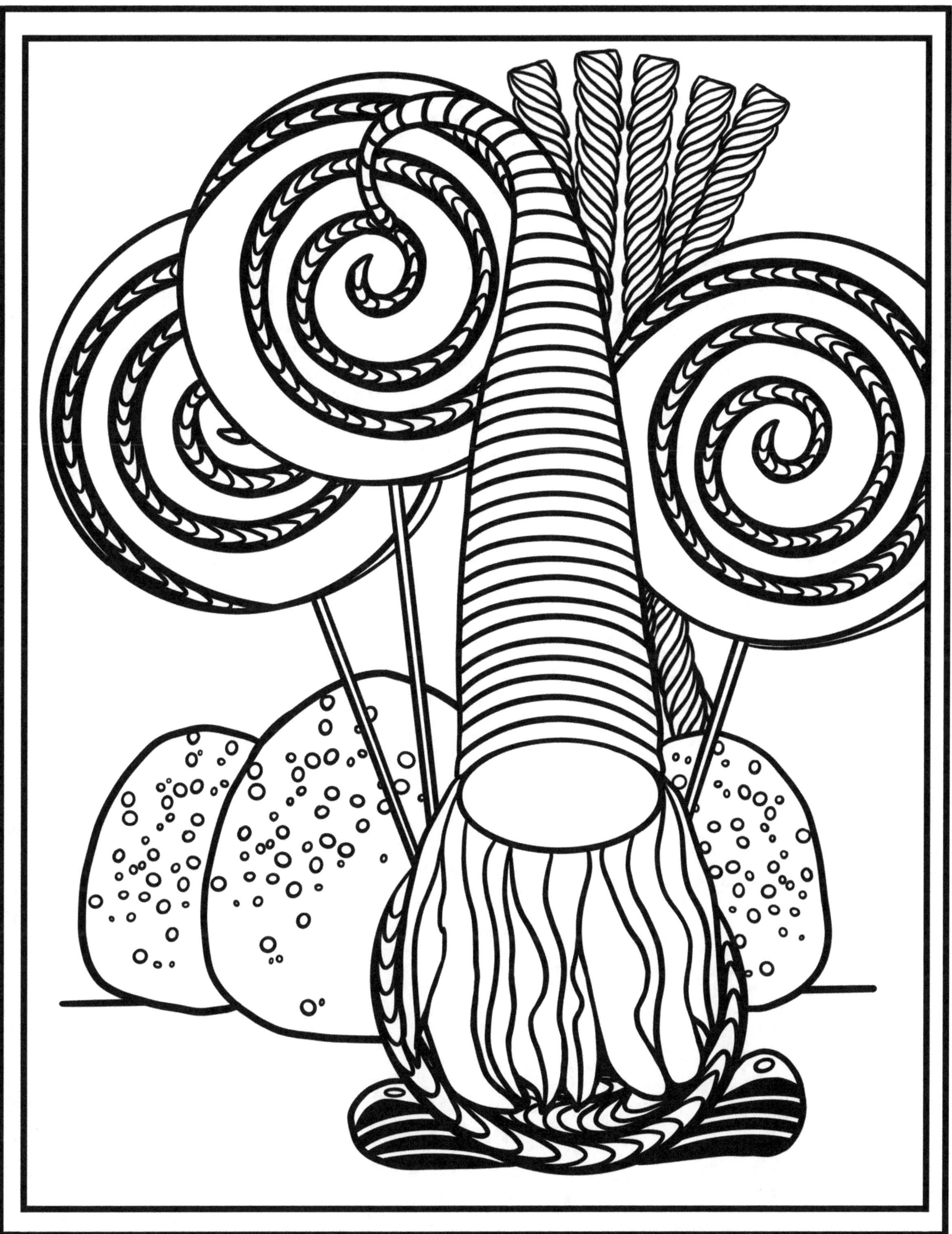

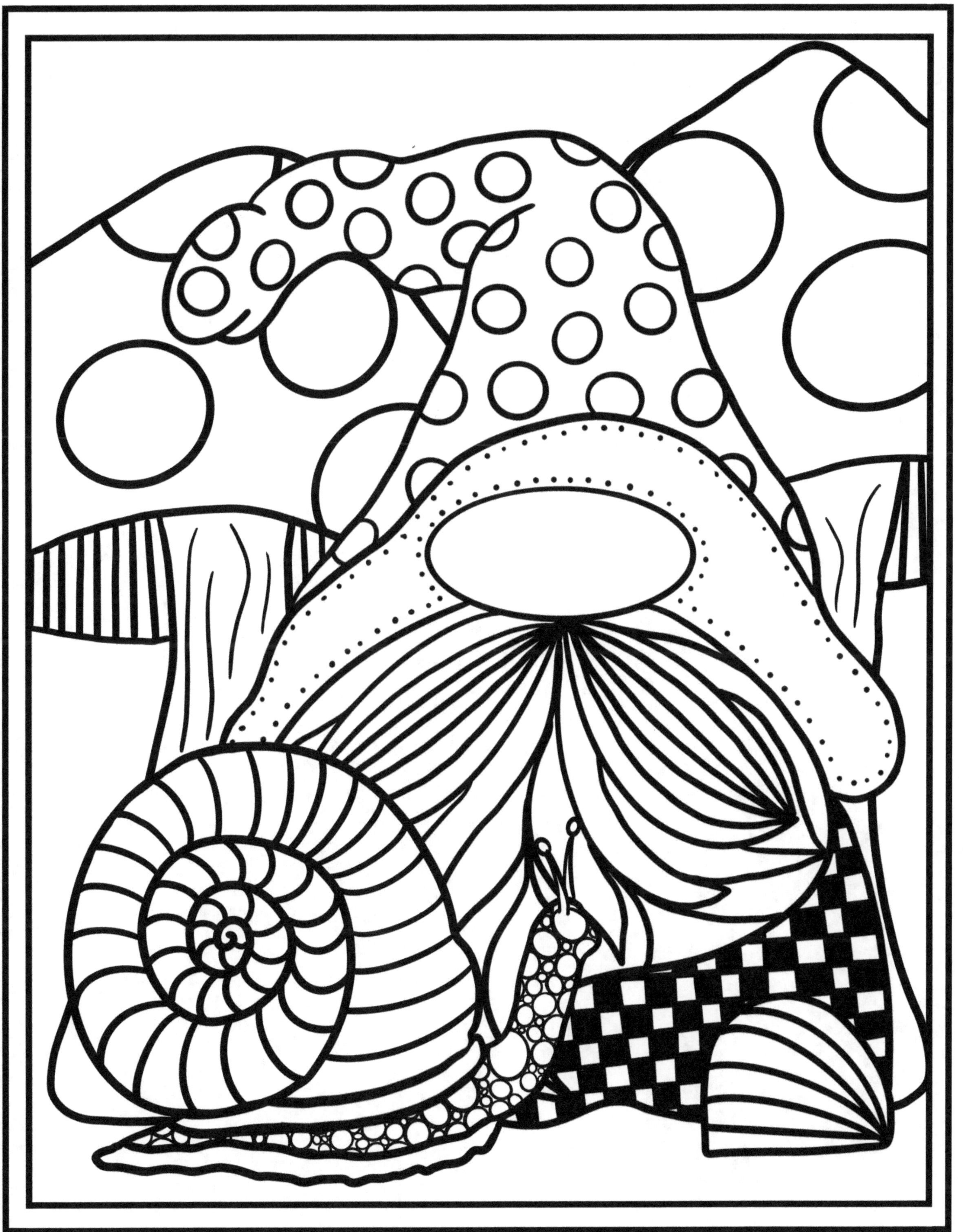

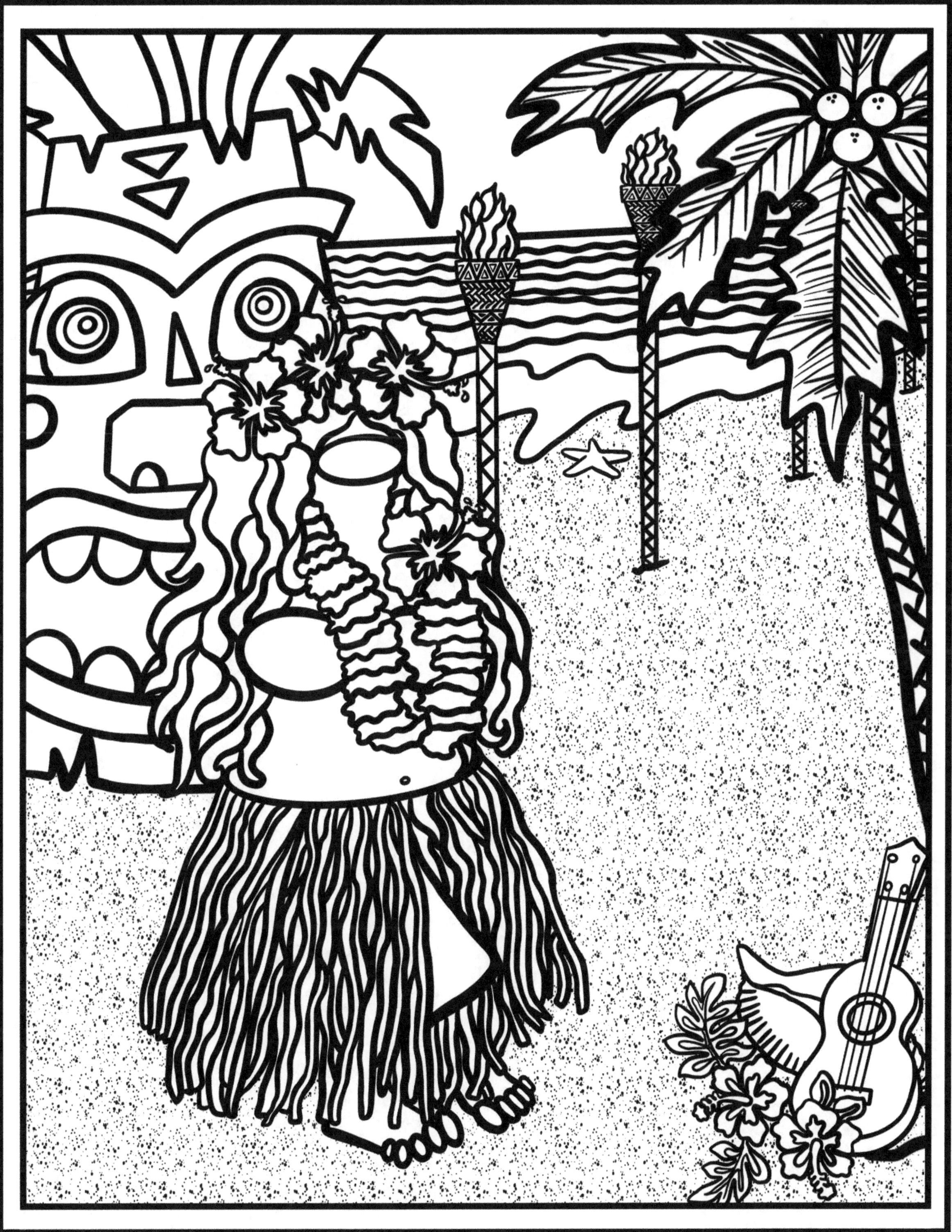

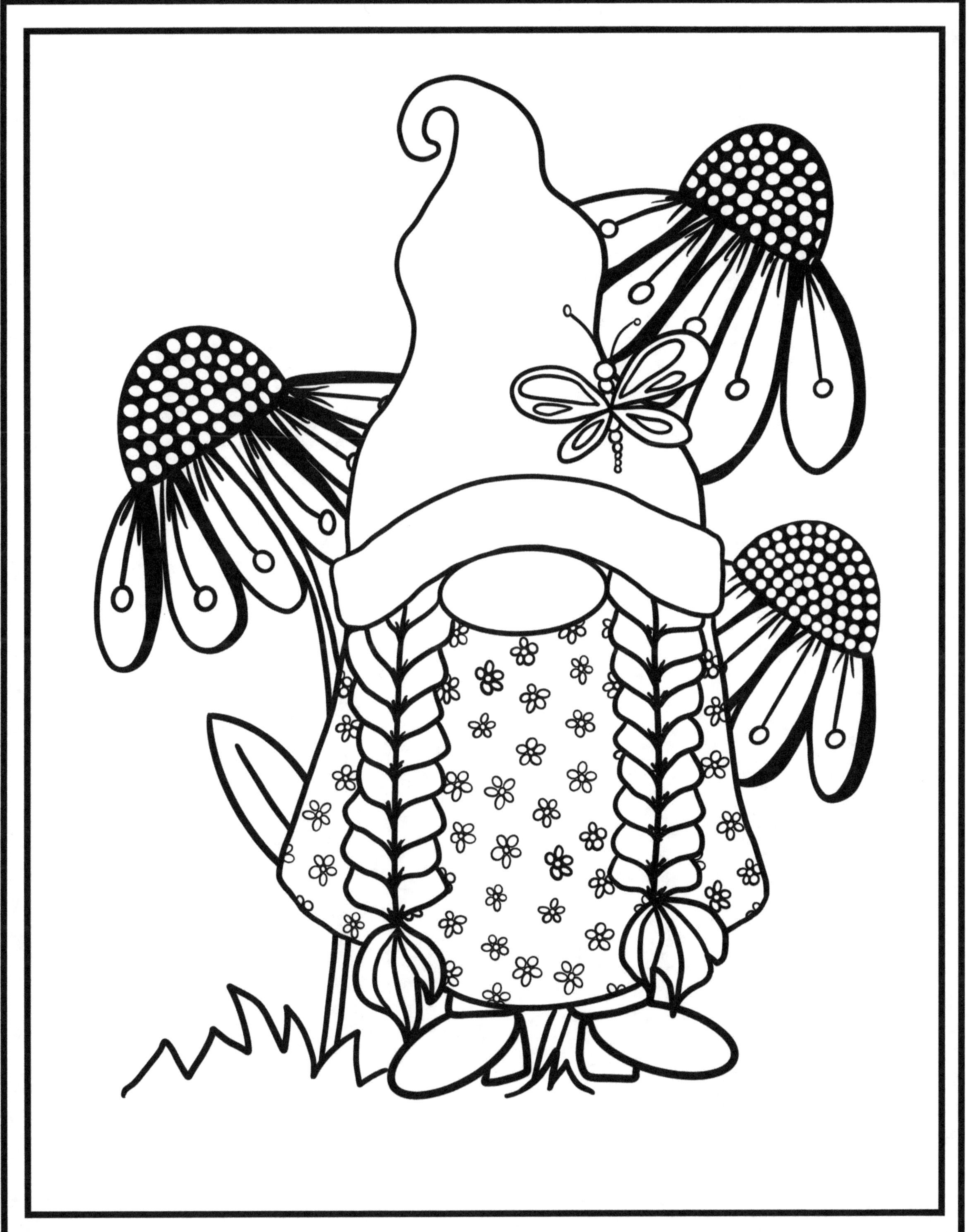

For more coloring fun,
check out the next
two volumes of
The Best Gnome Coloring Book
series.

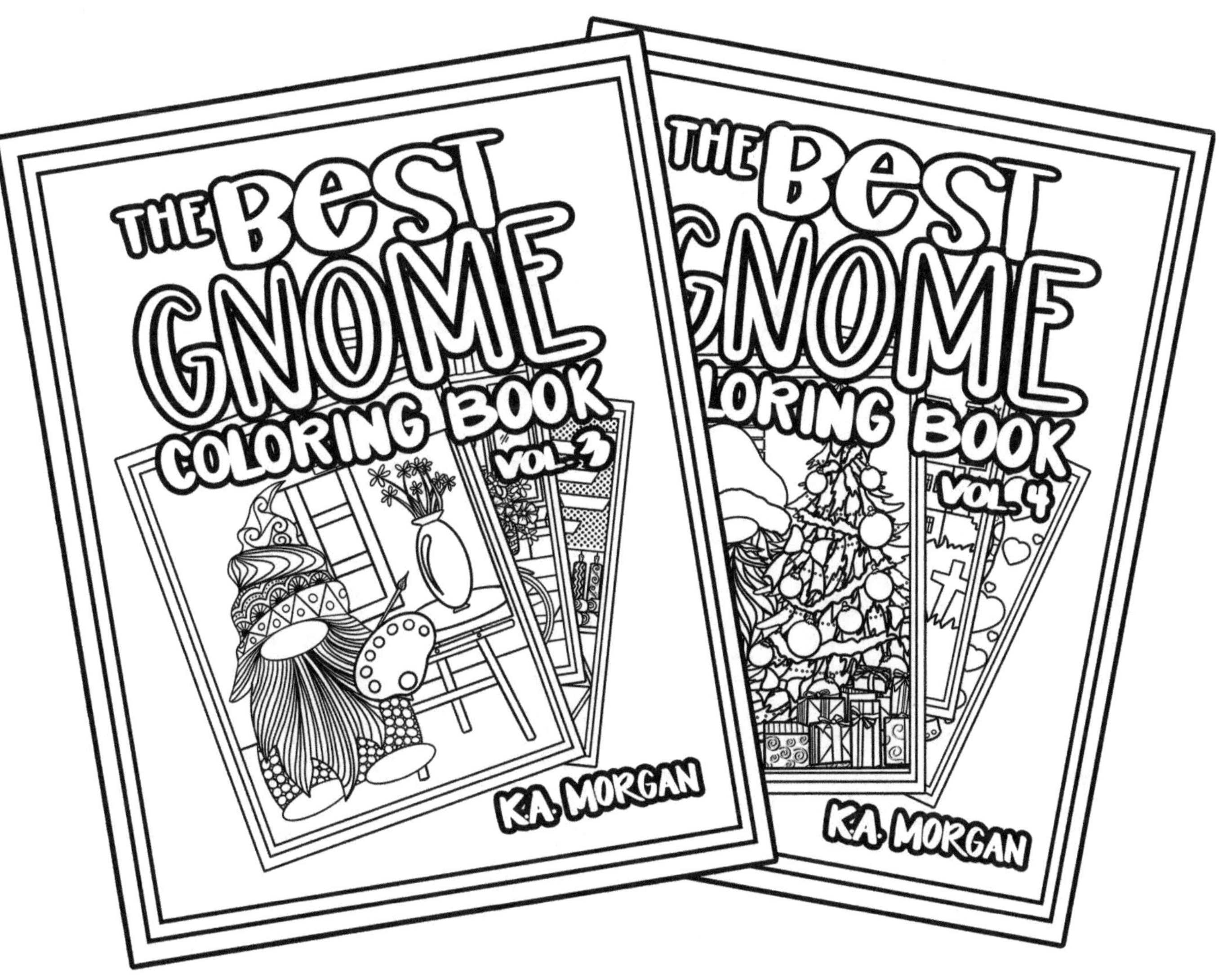

— FREE COLORING PAGE —

Send a photo or a scan of your *finished page(s) with your name to **kamorgan@inspirecreativeservices.com** and I will send you an exclusive free coloring page.

**May be featured on my website, on social media or in my newsletter with proper credit.*

www.ingramcontent.com/pod-product-compliance
Lightning Source LLC
LaVergne TN
LVHW080337110826
845155LV00027B/255

* 9 7 8 1 9 3 9 0 4 9 5 7 5 *